WHAT OTHERS HAVE SAID ABOUT TRUE WEALTH FORMULA

"I just want to thank you for never quitting on us. The True Wealth Formula message has never gotten stale! Over the last 10 years, ideas on investing and wealth have changed immensely and Hans Johnson's teachings have stayed relevant throughout."

—BRAD HARMSWORTH

"You were absolutely right when you said 'apply True Wealth Formula just one month and your bank account will look different'! I'm happy to say that for the first time I was able to take 40% of my income OFF the table and go to debt and my wealth account in addition to my 10% for Giving."

—NINA SHEPHERD

"Since implementing the TWF system, we have been able to pay off our credit card and save $8,000 into our wealth account without a pay increase. Thank you so much for putting together such a great system."

—DAVID EWING

"Just wanted to let you know that my team and I are studying your model because we are considering adopting it in our firm. As a fiduciary in the financial services industry for almost 20 years, what you teach is far and away different from what I studied (BBA in Finance) and trained at Morgan Stanley in 2000. I want to help set our clients up for financial independence not be another 98% financial advisor."

—CHRIS STALLINGS

"Hans Johnson is a hybrid of Dave Ramsey, Robert Kiyosaki, and Bruce Lee amplified to the nth degree. If you follow the system it works, it can't help but work. But, above and beyond the rules that are non-negotiable, Hans teaches you to think for yourself when it comes to money management, being a self-directed investor, and taking responsibility for your own... um, stuff. This curriculum is pure gold. Engage, follow directions, and live it up!"

—B.MTN.WOMAN (APP REVIEW)

"Budgeting in percentages was a mindset shift for me! I have always been 'good' with money, good saver, etc., but I want to be GREAT with money and have our money working harder for us!!! Now, I'm learning those skills! After being burned by the stock market in the past, I am feeling much more confident and empowered about investing in dividend-paying stocks and looking at our investments with a different lens... Our giving has also increased, and that feels great!"

—TINA HOLAN

"This app is really useful. From the content on investing to the articles on true wealth, whether it is to have fun, become more efficient, help others or even rise to the top, this app is sure to play a crucial role in your development. At the very least, I know it has improved how I manage and build my assets, how I handle risk and how I define true wealth."

—KEVIN JAASIEL (APP REVIEW)

"As workaholics, my wife and I always fall off the TWF bandwagon. But we've got our accounts, we've got our $1000 portfolio and we make small progress here and there. The beauty of TWF is that you can come back to it at any point, pick up where you are, and not have missed anything. This is truly the easiest formula to follow if you stay diligent and follow directions!"

—JEFFERY QUEEN

"We knew how to get out of debt and stay out, but holding onto and growing money is a whole different level. This app leads you step by step, not by someone making money from it but by people who already did it and know the ropes."

—JEN STRICKLAND (APP REVIEW)

"A revolutionary way to manage money which breaks down the steps into simple no-nonsense tasks. Takes the stress and hassles out of figuring out the current decisions. Best education app I have!"

—ABIGAIL BURTON (APP REVIEW)

"This has helped us immensely with our future financial health! A massive side benefit to the information and learning from this app has improved my marriage!"

—SHELLEY CALVER (APP REVIEW)

"TWF Rocks. Day one we had $237k in assets and $223k in liabilities while our Net was $14k. Today we have over $530k in assets and $441k in liabilities with a Net of $58k. We increased our income from $7k per month to $15k. We paid off over $34k in debt since starting TWF and cut $2,000 a month in fat. From the beginning of our journey with True Wealth Formula, we have given over $21,000 to the tithe. Thank you, Hans, you are incredible."

—MIKE GIBSON

"TWF has given us the confidence to invest for ourselves. Yesterday we used some of our own research along with suggestions from Hans' sample portfolio to invest in our own retirement accounts. It was so powerful to go in knowing that our strategy focuses on reducing risk. We put stops on everything and used the ND rules for position sizing. Thank you, Hans!"

—TIFFANY EWING

"This has been awesome for me and my family, especially that I now know I need to transfer funds between my account by percentages, it gets rid of your mind playing tricks on you. By using the percentages, I find it makes me more ruthless,

I transfer without that thought of indecision. I am also overjoyed to have a 'giving' account that keeps racking up—and have such great pleasure in tithing to those in need without missing the ratio that I need to give. Thank you so much Hans!"

—TED NORMAN

"The percentages make it so simple, not trying to add up specific numbers to come up with budgets, etc. It's simple! Everything about it is simple."

—ABIGAIL BURTON

"The TWF message has changed the future of our family without question. Prior to joining the TWF community, my wife and I were $212,000 in debt between a mortgage, a car loan, two personal loans, and a wide variety of credit cards. My debt payments required a $65,000 salary just so I could pay the minimums! Needless to say, we were drowning and were going further into debt each month. The most important lesson we learned through TWF is that you have to begin to think for yourself. We started running our own numbers and learned the strategy and the tactics for paying off debt and building TRUE wealth. In just 7 months, we have paid off over $35,000 worth of debt (from high-interest credit cards) and have actually begun investing in our future. The stress from the constant pressure of debt hanging over our heads is beginning to go away and we are on the path to becoming debt-free! Thank you Hans for changing our future!!"

—JORDAN KEEFE

"Thank you, Hans! I have done a lot of different 'money' programs but yours is in a league of its own with the empowerment it affords people!"

—MELODIE WILLIAMS

"We had subscribed to the program for almost a year while working on debt. Little did we know we had an ingenious, understandable and bluntly honest resource that perfectly meshes with the things we were already working on right at our fingertips! We are now immersed in TWF, learning and understanding the principles and formulas; separate accounts set up and being used, investing (what?!) and on our way to catching up to all the things we didn't know, and at 60! TWF is for any age and I know we will see results because the little sprouts are already popping up."

—SUZANNE HANDLEY

"The BEST training out there to show you how to get your money working for you. A step by step program that is easy to understand, implement, and takes all of the guesswork to save you time & keep you from learning things the hard way. The mistakes were made for us so that we only have to follow directions and start seeing RESULTS!!"

—JENNIFER WILLBURN

"My husband and I have been using this app and trainings that are offered for about a year and we are blown away by the quality of the information!!! It helped us more than

what we expected with specific formulas, and how to set up your financial family legacy goals. Very simple and easy to apply tools and it's always in the process of development and improvement. As soon as we applied what we are taught we got instant results. It's slowly changing our mindset to build generational wealth vs being just 'rich.' Hans and his family have high standards and values to help people!! THANK YOU!!!"

—OLGA MINKO

"Great app and the True Wealth Formula classes are profound. It's COMPLETELY changing our investment/wealth building strategies!"

—MELISSA SIEKS

"My husband and I only recently started implementing the True Wealth Formula system. Previously we really had no idea where our money was going and hundreds of extra dollars were getting blown month after month. We had no real system that helped us save and keep more of our money. Using your formula, we are telling our money what its purpose is and it gives us such a feeling of accomplishment! We now live on 60% of our income, and we used to barely make it off 100% of our income! We give 10% every month now, and we pay extra on our debt (20% of our income). We are finally diving in and following directions and it is awesome to see money growing in the bank and debt getting paid off faster! Thank you Hans for sharing your strategy for increasing your family's wealth, it has been a life-saver for us!!"

—JASON & DANA WINAND

"I was one of those people that didn't think it would work for me, didn't think I was smart enough, and ESPECIALLY didn't think it would really work, as I live outside the U.S. Well after taking a leap of faith, plugging into Hans' TWF course and Wealth Builder app has been a total game changer for me! I 'thought' I was good with money, however, making your money work for you and building wealth is a whole other skill that Hans teaches...and my goodness it WORKS, if you choose to APPLY it!! My mindset has totally changed, I get it and understand the concepts much more! You get ALL sides, the good, the bad, and the ugly. He teaches you what others DON'T want you to know. There is no sugar coating here!! Just honest real truth that will put you on the path to building true wealth! I started with over 120k in debt, now I'm debt free and have over 300k net worth (and growing)."

—HARRIETTE AMEKUEDI

"So many great practical tips. Take the emotions out of your decision making and live by rules that have been in existence for thousands of years but so few actually know them or how to apply. Hans is a passionate teacher and has built an awesome community of people learning, sharing and growing together."

—BRENIN RESTON

"Hans Johnson is by far one of the wisest men I've ever heard. I am grateful for the opportunity to learn from such an intelligent humble man willing to help others with the knowledge

that he has spent years acquiring. It's like getting the 'Cliff's Notes' to my financial future. Easy to learn and easy to implement. Thank you Hans for investing in my future!"

—KENDRA SWIGER

"This app and Hans are the real deal. He's the first true wealth building coach I have encountered. Notice that I did not say 'financial adviser,' as Hans sells nothing but how he has learned from experience. What built my trust in him is simply that he does not sell any financial instruments and that he is a good, solid family man."

—NOTENUF JAVA

"Hans Johnson is a master in building wealth and creating businesses. I have not found a better app or program that is filled to the brim with content you can put into action immediately."

—ELLIOT O

"I love the simple but comprehensive layout of this app. The creator has done a great job in making this an interactive app between himself and his clients. Already learning new things about wealth and I just started!"

—E GIUFFRE (APP REVIEW)

"This is my 3rd day with TWF and so far I can tell that Hans is literally the smartest person I know. His way of thinking and the wisdom he has just blows my mind. I'm on the 4th

Module right now, and I already have gained so much knowledge and understanding what is keeping me away from true wealth and how to increase my income. I'm so grateful for the opportunity that has been given to me to change the way my family sees the money."

—JANA MEIERE

"Todd and I are your typical, over-educated professionals with lots of letters after our names such as CPA and MBA. We have diligently paid into our retirement plans to create our 'retirement nest egg.' We also did the 'make more, spend more,' wondering why we weren't getting ahead. TWF changed our whole way of thinking about creating wealth and a legacy for our future and generations to come...not just retiring. After implementing TWF, we have paid off $40,000 in debt, making us consumer debt-free. It is a simple strategy that has transformed our financial approach and encouraged a financial discipline that we are passing on to our children, creating a legacy of wealth building."

—KELLY KENNEDY

"I am so very thankful to be able to be a part of this True Wealth Formula training! I am seeing breakthroughs in the last couple of years with my three oldest children. My 19-year-old son currently owns three rental properties due to me sowing into him this mindset. I have increased my business majorly by putting this mindset into action as well as my personal life. It's very encouraging to see my balance sheet/net

worth go up every month in a positive way! My relationship with my wife and children are so much better than they were five years ago! And having my finances in order has VERY much to do with it!! What would've taken me a lifetime to learn, took me about five years with this training!"

—GLENN BEACHY

"I'm blown away by the new information and principles for managing my money and wealth in such a way that is new to me in the financial world. It's opened my eyes and has given me an appreciation for what you do and how you have helped me so much. I'm continuing to learn and invest in your educational program. It's been life-changing for my life and family."

—DAVID MANLEY

"True Wealth Formula helped me to understand what 'Legacy' really means. While at the same time giving me strategies to plan, create, and leave a legacy for my kids."

—JACKIE O'QUINN

"I was lucky enough to sign up and join a group that Hans coached via calls and gave a much deeper level of understanding by building a solid foundation. Listening to the content over and over, then signing up for TWF Implementation program, I evolved to where I am now; have multiple streams of income, Consulting business, W2 income, Rental income, Hard Money loans (backed by real estate) and a Diversified

portfolio of Dividend-paying stocks. I am well on my way to Financial Freedom, please join me on this exciting journey."

—BRENDAN MORAN

"TWF message has definitely made an impact on our lives the last couple of years! We no longer think only about what money can do for us but how we can change the world with our money. This new paradigm in our mindsets has changed the way we manage money, invest, and also our vision for building a legacy for our family! Thank you, Hans, for your diligence, expertise, and advice! Can't wait to get a 'Signed' copy of your book!"

—TOM HASE

"In two months from purchasing TWF, I have implemented my ratios and I AM telling my money where to go. For the first time in 28 years, I am debt free and I have money in all of my accounts. Prior to TWF I was living paycheck to paycheck, broke and in debt. This program has changed everything. It changed the way I think about money, it's educated me on how money and the financial laws work. I have a vision for my money and future and I am seriously a new person. Hans says 'you can't NOT generate wealth with this program,' even if you apply the first part you will. It's not just that, it's the renewing of my mind and the old stinky habits which kept me STUCK for years and years. Finally, I have FREEDOM!!"

—RACHEL SHEPHERD

"TWF has given my family so much. My eyes are now open to what is possible on a single income for our family of 7. I had lost hope about ever becoming financially independent but now I am excited and looking forward to that day. We, as a family, have paid off more than $100,000 of our mortgage. With TWF, I now understand why our family was struggling. Every dollar we earn is taken care of so much better than ever before. It has given us the rules to help educate our children where before all I knew was save money, spend money, and then save it again. 'Get your money working for you, instead of you working for it.' This phrase has not only changed our minds but saved our life. Hans, you will never know how much this program has helped our family and to what extent but I want to thank you for investing in us. We are truly grateful. The Lord has really been in your heart to share your knowledge and help so many families across the world. Thank you, thank you, thank you from the bottom of my heart. We are forever grateful to you."

—FRANK AND CATHY KUHN

"TWF was the key that unlocked the vault and accelerated the war on debt program for us. In 5 years we paid off $500,000 in debt becoming debt-free. This allowed my husband to resign from the USMC and relocated our family internationally to my home country of Australia. We have remained debt-free since and we are now glad to be back, a part of the community so we can start our life after debt plan and create True Wealth for ourselves and our 4 teenagers."

—JANINA VASQUEZ

"My favorite thing about TWF is the app on my phone. I am a designer so I am not the best with financial spread sheets. Putting a number in expenses/mortgage payments to see where you stand on actual debt and payments is great. The calculator makes you realize how much you really are spending on interest and that motivates me to work at paying down my mortgage. Love it! Also I loved the financial talks by Hans at the seminars. I was a saver but then got out of the habit as my career changed but now I am working on getting back on track and want financial freedom."

—JAIMA EMMERT

"Being a member of the Wealth Builder family has truly changed our vision from how we look at our expenses to how we manage our growth. Prior to joining, let's just say we were normal, spending here, paying bills, paying down debt, adding debt, putting some in savings and wanting freedom. In short one step forward and one step back. By following the TWF System our vision has become clearer and we are moving forward to achieve financial independence. Since beginning of March 2019 we have developed a solid plan and reduced our debt by over $7k and not added any additional. We've grown our wealth account every month (while paying down additional debt) and creating an investment strategy that is returning 18% on our seed money! I now look at our household and finances as I would a business. TWF has truly changed our mindset towards our financial goals, Hans, and I would like to thank you and your brilliant team for taking the time and putting together an amazing program!"

—JASON AND LINA STAGGS

"I wanted to thank you for your knowledge. I have finally finished the course and am working on getting rid of my depreciating assets in addition to opening my investment account. Looking forward to picking my CFA and getting my money working for me instead of me working for my money!! This has totally changed how I look at managing my money."

—KELLEY BURKETT

"Great changes started to happen after the TWF classes. I have started to become master of our money and not a slave. It really is a total reprogramming of the way we think about money and what we should be doing with it. My husband and I found ourselves in almost the same amount of consumer debt we had back in 2009. At that time though, we didn't know what to do, so we claimed bankruptcy and never addressed the real money issues. I got a hold of FSTW book and couldn't put the book down. I started implementing what was in the book about finances Jan. 2018 and paid off almost \$30,000 by December 2018. All the while, we invested in the TWF 10% sample portfolio, grew our other accounts, went to 6 Dani Johnson events, vacations, and helping the poor and getting kids out of sex trafficking. Things really got more exciting when I implemented TWF. My accounts grew even more now that the money was on auto-pilot. We decreased our consumption and raised our income to achieve the double compounding effect with the debt elimination. TWF is an awesome system to put in place to achieve financial freedom, security and fulfillment in life. It opened my eyes to how much I was a slave to my money."

—SARAH HALL

TRUE WEALTH FORMULA

TRUE WEALTH FORMULA

HOW TO MASTER MONEY,
LIVE FREE & BUILD A LEGACY

HANS JOHNSON

First published in India by

SANAGE
PUBLISHING HOUSE

Sanage Publishing House

TRUE WEALTH FORMULA

How to Master Money, Live Free & Build a Legacy @ 2020
Hans Johnson. Original English language edition published by Scribe Media
815-A Brazos Street, Suite #220 , Austin, TX , 78701, United States.
Arranged via Licensor's Agent: DropCap Rights Agency. All rights reserved.

ISBN 978-9-3949-2453-6 *Paperback*

978-1-5445-0612-8 *Ebook*

CONTENTS

ACKNOWLEDGMENTS

To my beautiful, dilligent wife Dani. You have been a treasured gift and blessing to me. Your passionate heart and relentless spirit have forever influenced not just our family but the lives of millions. Thank you for your unwavering dedication to our family and for never giving up, even during the most difficult of times. Thank you for always believing in me and in this message. Without you there would be no TWF. You truly are a Proverbs 31 woman and you will always be beautiful to me.

To our kids, Arika, Cabe, Roman, Micah, and Kristina. You guys are all just amazing people. Sharing life and learning from you has been a priceless gift. Thank you for your humor, your perseverance, and your warrior's hearts. You are the next generation. The world truly is yours and you have what it takes to overcome all things. I believe in you.

To my mom and dad. Thank you both for choosing life, for always doing your very best, for always encouraging and believing in me. I love you both and it is an honor to be your son and carry on your legacy.

To the Creator. There is no one like you, no grace like your grace, no mercy like your mercy, no love like your love. Thank you for your breath of life, for your eternal wisdom, and patience. Thank you for Fathering me and teaching me your ways and higher law. You are the true source of all freedom, security, and fulfillment. May this book honor you, your ways, and your eternal laws.

To the many mentors, guides, and teachers that have inspired us in this life journey. Thank you for being willing to share your knowledge and encourage our growth.

To the editors and project managers who patiently helped me organize my thoughts and get this book finally done, I and many others are grateful for you and the work you do.

To our incredible clients, thank you for your dedication to the principles in this book and to making a much-needed difference in this world. Your encouragement, support, and feedback have helped refine and spread the TWF message in ways that would never have been possible without you. I am forever humbled and grateful.

DISCLAIMERS

Writing this book has been a terrifying experience. To take on a complex topic such as investing or wealth-building, and put it into words that make any sense, with the goal of it not becoming immediately obsolete, or not stating something incredibly foolish, is a humbling experience. My hope is you'll embrace the larger search and meaning behind TWF while also benefiting from its specific strategies and tactics.

Please always check the TrueWealthFormula.com website for updates, revisions, or changes to this book, PDF worksheets, bonus content, or the TWF system in general. Most importantly, you will want to download and subscribe to our Wealth Builder mobile app for the latest evolution of TWF as we continue to develop and refine our philosophy and algorithms through technology.

You should also know that although I am the passionate author of this book, and while I've had some truly incredible life and business experience, I wouldn't call myself an expert on this topic. There's just too much to learn and apply. Life and the markets are volatile and they have quite a knack for humbling people much smarter than I.

Additionally, I've specifically and almost exclusively used the "he" pronoun in this book for simplicity reasons only. Feel free to substitute it with whatever you feel it should be. TWF is not a pronoun dependent concept or system, so please make it personal to you.

Finally, please know that I am just a private investor, business owner, husband, and father who is sure to make many more life mistakes before my beloved eternal dirt nap arrives. I am not a licensed financial advisor, CPA, attorney, or therapist. You should always do your own due diligence and consult a qualified professional concerning your specific situation.

Enjoy the journey, my friend.

CHAPTER 1

ORIENTATION

WHY YOU SHOULD READ THIS BOOK

A famous celebrity who's struggling to account for his "missing $650 million" has been in the news recently—an *ultra-high* income earner who relied on "trusted" managers who either misadvised him or couldn't rein in his out-of-control lifestyle and spending. It's a real mess with a lot of finger-pointing and lawsuits. The story perfectly outlines the reason for this book.

Who's the victim? Who are the villains?

It's easy to look at famous people and think: How stupid! What an idiot! That would never happen to me. To be clear, there are *massive* pressures public figures live under that only end up exacerbating deeper problems. Lack of privacy alone is a huge issue. In the celebrity's case, a $2 million monthly spending habit couldn't fill the void.

For anyone who's ever thought, "If I could just make more money, my problems would be solved and I'd be happy," this book is for you.

The cause of the famous celebrity's misfortune?

No one—neither him, nor his top attorneys or financial advisors—seemed to understand the difference between cash-flow and non-cash-flow assets, which is something this book will drill into your head ad nauseam. But the problem goes much deeper than that.

So who's to blame?

To be sure, there's plenty of blame to go around, but, in the end, there's only one person with ultimate responsibility.

The reality is: *no one will do for you what you are not willing to do for yourself.* That means you, and you alone, are responsible for your financial situation and well-being, or lack thereof. No one owes you anything.

If that statement offends you, then you might as well put this book down now because, as you'll soon see, understanding and coming to agreement with this uncomfortable truth is the beginning of your freedom. I had to confront this reality within myself, and it wasn't easy, believe me! It's always easier to blame others, especially when we feel wronged or taken advantage of.

And what about the family who's barely making ends meet? How do they break free of financial slavery and start building wealth? This book answers their concerns, too.

I've spent a great deal of my life working to answer these and many other questions about money and wealth for myself, my family, and our clients.

True Wealth Formula is the outcome of a personal journey of self-discovery, sorting through the ungodly amount of financial information and misinformation out there, and developing a reliable system that produces repeatable, automated results.

Why did I write this book? To answer the age-old questions: How do I become free? How do I turn money into my slave instead of being a slave to money?

The information shared in this book isn't taught in school. It's what only a few of the world's most elite Wealth Builders know.

Welcome to the True Wealth Formula, your roadmap and blueprint to personal freedom. Enjoy the journey!

THE VALUE OF WORK

I started my first business at the age of eight in Kona, on the Big Island of Hawaii, where I grew up.

We were poor, living on welfare, and needed extra cash to buy food, school supplies, and other necessities. I grew up without a father. My mother was a struggling single mom, and about every three to six months we'd have to move. Though we had food on the table thanks to food stamps, the situation was always volatile, with my younger brother and I often sleeping on box-spring mattresses on the lanai, the covered porch. That's when I started making leis after school.

I'd come home, pick flowers from nearby plumeria trees, and make the traditional Hawaiian garlands of welcome. Then I'd walk around the village in an aloha shirt with the leis hung on a bamboo pole and sell them to tourists.

Some people might think that's a terrible thing for a little kid to have to do, but for me it was a powerfully liberating experience. Not only did I have the chance to roam the streets—what more could a kid want?—I also learned some extremely valuable life lessons.

It didn't take me long to appreciate the value of hard work: that if I wanted something bad enough and was willing to work for it, I could achieve it. It was an opportunity to learn the basics of sales and how to handle rejection—not everyone wanted to buy my flower necklaces, and I'd often get shooed away.

Because my product had a short shelf life, I had to learn time management and figure out when to discount the price. Even though I was growing up in an unstable, poor environment, I was discovering the vital skills of entrepreneurship, persistence, and adaptability.

Not many young people today have the opportunity to get their minds opened up that way. I was fortunate to have a mom who believed in me. Again, not every young kid gets that kind of experience. I will forever be grateful for her encouragement.

By the time I was twelve, because of instability at home, I was bouncing between living with my mom, my grandparents, and the dad of a friend of mine. It was then that I first remember dreaming about financial independence.

I promised myself that someday, somehow, I'd become a millionaire. I knew I didn't want to raise my kids the way I'd grown up. By the time I was sixteen, I was living on my own permanently.

To say I had a short childhood and learned how to survive early in life would be an understatement, but I've always tried to focus on the positives. It was only later, when I dealt with the lingering effects of a poverty mindset, that I realized how my underlying fear of being poor was affecting my relationship with money and others.

Our mindset, programming, and belief systems shape our perspective in life, and they can become a major liability in the wealth-building process. It's a topic we'll discuss in detail later.

THE #1 KEY TO WEALTH

The chaos of my childhood had another positive outcome—martial arts training.

The training gave me much needed stability, focus, and self-discipline. I studied with a man named Damien who, though I didn't know it initially, was a millionaire.

In our training sessions, Damien would talk about the difference between the 99 percent and the 1 percent. He said that ninety-nine percent of the population look for the easy way out. Only one percent never quit.

I started spending more time with Damien. He became a father figure and my first wealth mentor and is a close friend to this day. I'm grateful for everything I learned from Damien.

Damien knew I was motivated to make money. I always asked him questions about success, and one day he shared a secret with me: he said the *number one key to wealth is to get your money working for you instead of you working for your money.*

I wrote down those words when I first heard them. A timeless truth and seed of wisdom had been planted deep in my heart and mind. It would take many years of watering and sifting to reach its full potential.

WORKING HARD ISN'T ENOUGH

Days before graduating high school, my best friend Chris helped me land a job as a commercial diver for an underwater construction company. I loved it. I was the youngest diver on the team. It was challenging work and suited my introverted nature. I worked crazy hours—fifty to sixty hours a week—and made what I thought at the time was a great income. I was finally able to start my journey of saving money and thinking more seriously about financial freedom.

A guy named Miles was the senior diver who earned the top salary. He'd been a deep-sea habitat diver in the

North Sea, where he lived underwater for weeks at a time. Whenever one of us young guys had a problem, we went to Miles. We called him the "underwater MacGyver" and looked up to him. He represented the pinnacle and goal we all wanted to achieve. (*MacGyver* was an old TV show about a guy who could creatively get himself out of any situation, no matter how impossible.)

Over time, I realized that Miles worked six days a week and lived on the cheaper side of the island, where houses were affordable. During the week, he camped out in the back of his old pickup truck, and Saturday evenings he drove two hours to see his wife and one-year-old son. Sunday night he'd drive back to our side of the island to be at work again Monday morning.

I knew I didn't want to live like that. Although only in his mid-thirties, Miles looked like he was fifty because of the environmental stresses commercial diving puts on the body.

Slowly it dawned on me that this wasn't a career path for me. It made no sense to work that hard just to struggle. I didn't want to reach the pinnacle of my career and look like I had it together, but was really only living paycheck-to-paycheck with no time for my family.

I started seeing things differently. Having had a questioning nature since I was a kid, I've always asked why things were the way they were. I've never been afraid to challenge the status quo. I thought about entrepreneurship and having my own business again. I was eighteen, and it was the last time I worked for someone else.

THE WOMAN

Around this time, I had met a high energy gal named Dani, a couple years older than me, who had started a new business that took her from homeless to making $10,000 a month. At the time, my mind couldn't even conceive of that kind of cash, but there was an opportunity to learn what she was doing, and this powerful young woman became my business coach. I was totally sold and committed to learning, attending every seminar, listening to training audios every waking moment, learning how to sell and speak in front of people, which was something I was absolutely terrified of. For the first time in my life I had hope and a vision, and Dani was (and still is today) one of the world's best at training and motivating others to succeed.

Then something very unexpected happened: Dani and I fell in love, moved to California, got married, and had a family. *What the heck—how did that happen*?! Life was moving too fast for this simpleminded beach kid. The stress was high as I felt the weight, pressure, and responsibility of being a young (and clueless) husband and father.

As the years and business experiences passed by, I remembered my dream of financial independence, not seeing my kids have to grow up the way I did, and desperately wanting to succeed in my marriage and in life. I remembered what Damien had said and started thinking seriously about "how to get our money working for us." But before we could do that, we needed to make some *extra* money.

How was I going to earn money? How could I break the poverty cycle of living paycheck-to-paycheck and start saving discretionary income? We were making a *great* income from our business activities, but we weren't saving anything or building any true wealth. How could we get our money to work for us instead of always working for our money? Was there a system for doing this and, even more importantly, could the wealth-building process be automated and made fail-proof?

Finding answers to those questions turned into a lifelong journey of introspection, experimentation, and investigation into the immutable laws of wealth—defining true wealth, attaining it, keeping it, and making it grow.

These are the issues that lie at the heart of this book. There's an endless amount of money, success, and investing information out there, but most of it seems to fall short of providing a solid foundational strategy with specific steps to follow.

I was looking for a formula, something proven and tested, something "evergreen" with staying power, not just another fad. This book is the result of years of refining that system and it will teach you what you need to know to implement this formula in your life so that you and your family can experience *both* financial freedom and inner fulfillment.

THE BIGGER PICTURE

If you follow the steps outlined in this book, no matter what your background, you can become wealthy. True Wealth Formula (TWF) is both a framework for thinking and a master wealth-building strategy. It integrates everything we've learned over the years from living in poverty to living an amazing life of abundance and financial freedom.

While the majority of this book focuses on core strategic wealth-building principles and techniques, it also explores the meaning of true wealth itself.

Financial success is a means to an end. *Defining that end is important, but it's also personal, something each of us must do for ourselves in our own way.*

Unfortunately, defining wealth or success is something very few people ever take the time to do. We chase after a goal our whole lives but rarely stop or slow down long enough to ask: What am I striving for? Is this my dream or someone else's dream that I've been sold and programmed into accepting?

Keeping an eye on the big picture is as important as paying attention to the bottom line. This book will help you do both. It's both a manual for creating wealth and a philosophy for living a fulfilling and successful life. Indeed, TWF is a comprehensive *life-building* system, because if you make money but lose your soul, life becomes truly miserable.

MONEY DOESN'T BUY...

Growing up poor and then struggling as a young entrepreneur, husband, and father, I focused on business and money early in life. Only later did I begin to understand that there's a lot more to wealth than money.

When all our needs were taken care of, I had to face the question: *what next*? That's when I started thinking about the concepts of wealth and freedom more deeply.

In our journey towards true wealth, it's critical that we start with the end in mind and ask ourselves: *what would we do with our time if we had all the money we needed*? We'll revisit this question later.

We live in an age where people have more luxuries and are more prosperous than ever before in history. At the same time, many are more miserable than ever, which begs the question: *how much money does it take to feel happy and successful*?

A recent Princeton University study on the correlation between money and happiness addressed this issue. At what point, the study asked, does a person stop getting the same bang for the buck for each additional dollar earned? The answer was approximately $75,000 a year. That figure varies, of course, depending on where you live. In San Francisco, $75,000 doesn't go nearly as far as it does in other parts of the country.

What's interesting about the study is that once a person is living well, has enough money to pay the bills, and is enjoying life, having more money doesn't necessarily make him much happier. There's a big difference between the quality of life at $37,500 and $75,000, but according to the study, there's only marginal improvement in happiness between $75,000 and $150,000. Beyond a certain point, doubling your income doesn't necessarily double your happiness.

It's been said that money can't buy happiness. However, it appears that it can, but only up to a certain point. Then it has diminishing returns. *In some cases, happiness can even decrease with rising income.*

We've experienced both sides: we've been rich, and we've been poor. Though I certainly prefer being rich, I no longer delude myself into believing that having more money will bring more happiness. Quite often and strangely, more money equals more burden.

MONEY VS HAPPINESS QUADRANT

To solve this long-standing paradox and conflict, I want to introduce you to a diagram I call the Money vs Happiness Quadrant.

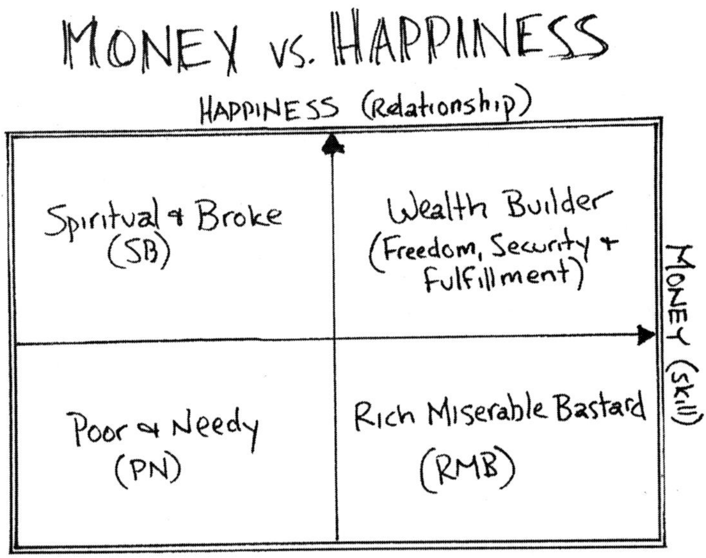

Nearly all of life comes down to two key areas: *money* and *relationships*. The grid presents four types of people relative to the priority they place on money and relationships in their lives.

The horizontal or x-axis represents material growth or money. The vertical or y-axis represents spiritual growth or happiness. The four quadrants are the four positions or life experiences people find themselves in.

On the left of the diagram are the positions of not having enough money or resources; on the right are the positions of a person who is financially well-off.

The top half are the positions that value relationships, love, contentment, spiritual strength, and fulfillment. At the bottom are the positions of being more concerned with ourselves, projects, things, and material possessions.

THE RICH MISERABLE BASTARD (RMB)

The person who occupies the lower right quadrant has money and material goods and often needs to show off his riches and accomplishments. He is what I affectionately call the Rich Miserable Bastard, or an RMB for short. I know that term is offensive to some, but I call it what it is because I've lived that life and it sucks.

An RMB lives according to society's expectations of what it means to be happy and successful. He buys nice cars and wears expensive clothes, or *he's so focused and stressed out on achieving his next major objective that he never enjoys or finds fulfillment in the present or the success he's already achieved*. Generally, he values status, material possessions, recognition, and achievement more than people and relationships.

A Mirage in the Desert

Often the RMB learns to focus on what he is good at, like driving projects and getting things done, but not on maintaining relationships. In extreme cases, he leaves a path of destruction in his wake, with the people closest to him feeling used and abused. He may have little self-awareness or rationalize his behavior as a survival mechanism or he believes he's always right.

At the root of the RMB's drive is *fear*. He's never satisfied. Every time he accomplishes a goal believing it will bring him happiness, it slips away like a mirage in the desert, while another distant goal or challenge takes its place. The RMB lives in a lonely prison. He may look like he's got it all together on the outside, but deep down he's insecure and miserable.

In some cases, an RMB does value and care deeply about people close to him, but he's just better at driving projects than managing relationships. Relationships create stress.

So, much to his own eventual detriment and misery, *he tends to focus on things he thinks he can control and that give him a feeling of accomplishment.* This was my personal struggle for many years. Because of fear, past experiences, and underlying heart issues, I often isolated myself and communicated in a passive-aggressive, unhealthy way, which was destructive to myself and others.

Compared to What?

If you think you can't possibly be a Rich Miserable Bastard because you're not "rich," you might want to think again. By almost any relative standard, if you live in a modern society and have running water and electricity, you are living extravagantly compared to many people today and certainly when compared to living standards over the course of human history. Today, even with the most modest of living circumstances, we literally live like kings and queens!

THE POOR AND NEEDY

In the lower left quadrant is the poor and needy person, the PN, who is the opposite of an RMB. Most of us start out in life that way. We go to school, get a job, and have a lot of debt—credit cards, student loans, etc.—or we jump from one job to another. We're not making ends meet and often rely on others for some kind of financial support or assistance.

Some healthy, able-bodied people get caught in an entitlement trap and never break out of the PN quadrant. *They spend their entire lives feeling someone owes them something and never learn to stand on their own two feet and support themselves. They remain dependent, either on family, friends, or government social-services programs. They never take full responsibility for their lives, preferring to blame others for their lack of progress.* Getting a temporary hand up is one thing. We've all had a bad break or fallen on tough times, but we should be doubling down, working twice as hard to get back on our feet and independent again as quickly as possible. Contrary to what some might believe, physical labor and effort are good for mental health. Being productive builds momentum and strength and compounds in many good ways.

THE SPIRITUAL AND BROKE

The top left quadrant is the person who's spiritually focused but broke, the SB. You may know people like that. I do. They're sometimes "salt-of-the-earth" types whose lives are driven by a worthy cause, or they're committed to an issue that is more important than their personal concerns. They are outwardly focused and often in the business of helping others via nonprofit or church-related activities. They often struggle financially and survive by "raising support" or getting help from friends and family. SBs are often happy and fulfilled, even if they can't pay their bills on time.

People who are genuinely called to a purpose of helping others are essential to society. Historically, they played a critical role in supporting widows, orphans, the handicapped, and those who were *physically* unable to work and earn a living. In many cases though, SBs have entitlement thinking and excuses similar to PNs. At the root of this often lies a belief system of judgment, rationalization, or entitlement about...you guessed it, money. In other cases, they make sacrifices that lead to personal and financial ill health and need to embrace the TWF marketplace mindset and skill development covered in this book.

THE WEALTH BUILDER

On the top right quadrant is a person who has Freedom, Security, and Fulfillment, the FSF or Wealth Builder. It's the sweet spot or target zone for True Wealth Formula.

Created deep within the spirit and soul of every human being, regardless of nationality, race, culture, or religion, is an innate desire for freedom, security, and fulfillment. No one wants to be oppressed and controlled by someone who dictates what they can do, think, or say, whether it's another person or an authoritative, overreaching government.

The most essential freedoms are freedom of thought, expression, speech, movement, privacy, and to be secure in your person and property. Other desirable freedoms include being able to determine your career path, decide whom you associate with, and have the opportunity to improve your financial standing.

It's important to understand that freedom and rights are not the same. Being free to do what you want does not mean someone owes you anything. *Freedom requires being responsible for your actions and not transgressing on another person or their property.* It requires a degree of uncertainty and risk, which is often in conflict with security, but in a free society, freedom is the higher priority and must be protected above all else.

We all want security. None of us wants to live in a war-torn country or a neighborhood with drive-by shootings. We all want to walk down the street safely at night and not live in terror of a lone-wolf attack or an oppressive regime. The desire for security, like the desire for freedom, is universal, and financial resources play a big part in having it.

Another important aspect of security is having confidence in who you are. Insecurity about yourself, whether through envy, jealousy, or unhealthy self-esteem, makes us and those around us miserable.

The final F in FSF is for fulfillment. Having a purpose gives meaning to our lives, especially when our purpose is greater than just satisfying our immediate personal needs and goals. *Fulfillment is probably the most important component of happiness.* It's much more than feeling accomplished or being recognized by peers or our social group. It's something that comes from a deep well of spiritual identity, strength, and contentment, from quality relationships and from contributing to others' lives, as well as our own personal growth.

THE PARADOX

Wherever people fall on the continuum of money and happiness reveals their goals and who they are. If we sacrifice our health or the quality of our relationships in pursuit of money, we'll eventually end up miserable, no matter how successful we become. If we're more focused on others at the expense of our own personal needs, we may not be able to live in comfort or be of much help to others. If we're needy ourselves, our ability to make an impact in the world and influence others is limited. Sometimes the best way to help others is to first help ourselves, so we can give from a position of strength, not weakness.

The money versus happiness quadrant clarifies our choices and solves the long-standing religious paradox of the rich man versus the kingdom of heaven. There is a correlation between the two, but they are not interdependent: correlation and causation are not the same thing. *Money is not the solution to misery any more than it is the cause of it. We don't have to be poor and needy, or spiritual and broke, to focus on an important cause or quality relationships. And we don't need to be a miserable bastard to be rich. There is always another choice.* Our beliefs, priorities, and willingness to learn and work hard determine where we fall on the quadrant.

We can aim our sights toward the upper right quadrant and achieve freedom, security, and fulfillment if we want it bad enough. TWF never encourages sacrificing relationships or quality of life for temporary worldly riches. At the same time, it doesn't allow us to cop out by not pursuing our dreams or not applying ourselves in order to achieve and make a difference.

THE CURE

The cure to moving along the money axis is *skill development*. The cure to moving up the happiness axis is *spiritual development* and *relationships*. If we want more happiness, we need to spend more quality time with the Creator and those closest to us.

In most cases, with the exception of overly oppressive governments and physical or mental handicaps, a core belief system and victim identity are at the root of staying stuck and not moving towards the FSF quadrant of the Wealth Builder.

It takes a certain amount of unhappiness or discomfort to motivate us to do the things that will make us successful. Comfortable people don't usually have the drive to change, learn new skills, or challenge their thinking and belief patterns. If you're not currently in the Wealth Builder quadrant, and you want to experience a richer more fulfilling life, this book will be your roadmap on how to get there.

THE HIGHER PRIORITY

To the point of how important relationships are to our lives, a study was done that asked people what their biggest concern was before retirement. The answer...not having enough money. The study later followed up with the same people a couple years after they had retired, asking them the same question. The answer...*loneliness*. This ought to give us a sober reminder of what's most important in life.

The Wealth Builder values relationships above money, status, and accomplishments, and he develops an intuition of when his core relationships are out of whack and need attention. This doesn't mean he tries to please everyone; it just means he knows that without an active, healthy relationship with his Creator and those closest to him, he's just a Rich Miserable Bastard.

Now let's move along and continue to lay the foundation to our wealth-building system!

THE PARTHENON STRUCTURE

TWF is structured like the Greek Parthenon. When properly built, it gives us the blueprint for a wealth-building machine that will stand the test of time.

The most important part of any structure is its foundation. The bigger the building, the stronger and deeper the foundation must be. You cannot build a multistory high-rise on top of a shallow, weak, or compromised foundation. You may get away with it for a while and feel that you're cheating the laws of nature and physics, but cracks will soon start to appear. And when they do, the entire structure is at risk of collapse.

The same is true when it comes to personal finance and wealth-building. *If we want a financial structure that's stable and withstands the test of time, we have to build it on a solid foundation.*

The foundation of a 100-story building goes deep into the ground. Like an iceberg with most of its mass under water, we can't see it, but we know it's there. The same principle applies to the True Wealth Formula.

The foundation of the True Wealth Formula consists of knowledge of universal laws that have been true since the beginning of recorded time. I like to think of them as *natural laws* of the Creator. They are laws and principles that describe the way things work.

Gravity is an example of a natural law. It's a fact that gravity exists. Whether we believe in it or not makes no difference on its effect and impact on our daily lives. Even the person who has never heard of gravity, and has no concept of its existence or how it works, is affected by it every single day.

Financial laws and principles operate in a similar way. They impact our lives whether we are aware of or believe in them or not. They are always there, working for us or against us.

PATTERN RECOGNITION

A knowledge of history, specifically historical patterns, helps us make sense of the crazy world we live in. It empowers us to understand the context of our lives and is an important part of the foundation of our wealth-building system. The purpose of history is not to memorize names, places, and dates. It's to give us wisdom, insight, and understanding. For example:

Why do governments inflate their currency and run a debt-based economy rather than backing their currency with hard assets?

Why is debt sometimes considered a terrible thing, while at other times it's good?

What social beliefs have shaped our culture, perceptions, and mindsets, and how do they impact our individual lives?

What drives mass psychology, groupthink, and our default tribal responses even today?

Why do we repeat the same mistakes and forget the lessons of history?

How does all of the above impact the financial markets, and how do we capitalize on it and, just as importantly, protect ourselves from it?

To answer these and other questions, we need to study *historical trends* and *human nature* to understand why certain patterns keep repeating themselves. By looking at the way things were in the past, we discover insights into why they are the way they are today.

Even though on the surface things may appear different, they really aren't, because the *underlying psychology of people, including you and me, hasn't changed for thousands of years.*

Human behavior is also a natural law. Human beings, no matter how evolved or civilized a society becomes, still think and act like they have since the beginning of time. Unchanging human psychology drives our behavior and decisions and impacts financial markets and our investments. With all the knowledge, resources, and information at our fingertips, the overwhelming majority of people are still victim to poorly timed investment decisions driven by dominant emotions of fear and greed. *This will never change.*

A strong foundation for building true wealth includes a knowledge of history, familiarity with the ideas that have shaped culture, and an understanding of the natural laws of the Creator.

COMPONENTS OF THE MACHINE

In the Parthenon diagram, three pillars sit on top of the Foundation, supporting the capstone or roof.

In TWF, the three pillars are Debt, Income, and Assets. You can think of these pillars like pistons that drive the core engine of our wealth-building machine. The roof is our personal Legacy, which should be the driving purpose for creating our wealth structure.

The five parts of the True Wealth Formula are:

- the Foundation, consisting of knowledge of the Creator, natural laws and human nature, historical patterns, current trends, and our mindset
- a support pillar of Debt
- a support pillar of Income
- a support pillar of Assets

- a roof or capstone of Legacy

True Wealth Formula provides a master strategy for our lives and the wealth-building process. In the sections ahead, we'll discuss each of the five parts in depth.

WEALTH-BUILDING TOOLS

In addition to providing a roadmap to experiencing a life of freedom, security, and fulfillment, True Wealth Formula includes foolproof money-management and investing strategies.

In this book, you're going to learn how to:

- Reprogram your mind for wealth-building
- Eliminate your debt and experience freedom
- Develop power skills to survive and thrive in the new economy
- Understand the difference between how the wealthy manage money versus the poor and middle class
- Invest like the wealthy and build assets the right way
- Avoid being a victim of theft, fraud, or poor advice from financial experts and advisors
- Build a legacy that lasts and influences generations to come

Money is a tool. It can do a lot of good in the world, as

this book makes abundantly clear. It's an expression of our philosophy of life—money's function and how we use it can't be separated. Money communicates values.

Mindset is a critical part of wealth management. TWF values lifelong learning and a ruthless search for truth. When you adopt the TWF mindset of continual self-improvement and resilience, you truly do embrace a lifelong journey of adventure!

As I've said to many of our clients over the years, once you learn the TWF system and mindset, the world will never be the same. You will see the world with a new set of eyes and from a totally different point of view. You'll understand why things are the way they are, and instead of being frustrated, confused, and victimized, you'll jump into the game to win.

This book will give you everything you need, but you have to make the decision to learn, apply, and master what it teaches. *Remember this law: no one will do for you what you are not willing to do for yourself*! You have to step up to the plate and make the decision to master your own destiny and create your legacy. TWF will become your roadmap and blueprint. It will change your thinking and the trajectory of your financial life forever.

CHAPTER 2

FOUNDATION

True Wealth Formula is built on a foundation of knowledge, wisdom, and understanding. Without a solid foundation, the three pillars of mastering Debt, Income, and Assets would crumble and collapse like a weak building under stress. The deeper and stronger the foundation, the bigger and more stable the structure can become.

The following pages will introduce you to a mindset or a way of looking at things and perceiving and understanding the world around us. More importantly, TWF is a way of seeing ourselves, which has a critical impact on our financial success or failure.

I invite you on a journey of reprogramming your mind and brain...to challenge the status quo of how you see, perceive, and believe what you do. *If we want a different result with our money, we have to think differently*. The only way to think differently is to replace default programs with newer, more effective ones.

CONTEXT IS EVERYTHING

The foundation of True Wealth Formula is based on a personal journey of trial and error and self-discovery. It comes out of an intense curiosity about the world and from asking questions about why things are the way they are.

As mostly an introvert, I often examine my own life, behavior, and motivations in order to understand how what we do and believe affects our results. And I like to study history, not in the traditional sense of memorizing names, places, and dates, but as a marketer focused on historical patterns of human behavior and psychology.

I'm a curious person. In any situation, I like to take a step back and ask the bigger question. I prefer to start with the 30,000-foot view of things. *In the TWF mindset, context is everything.*

For example, if I want to understand why a certain government policy is the way it is, I take a broad look at the way the government functions. Then, because all government is ultimately a reflection of people, I look into what motivates human beings at a core level, starting with myself. This requires a level of brutal honesty most people just aren't comfortable with. In most cases, we get the government we deserve, not the one we want. I find that there's always a deeper reason why things are the way they are, so I keep backing up and asking the bigger question.

THE ONLY CONSTANT

History, as we've all been told, repeats itself. Things may not always look the same, but human beings, our core emotional makeup and what drives us psychologically, haven't changed in thousands of years. Human nature remains fundamentally the same and doesn't change.

If you want to understand what's going on in the world today, if you want to know why the financial system collapsed in 2008 and why it will eventually collapse again, if you want to understand economic cycles or geopolitical events occurring globally, then *you have to take a good, long look at human nature.*

So how does one understand human nature? You begin with yourself. What is *my* nature? How do I react when I don't succeed at something or when I make a costly mistake? Who or what do I want to blame? Who am I looking for to rescue me, give me a handout or for help? What do I think needs to change in order for me to get where

I want to go? Why do I have the thoughts I have, believe the things I believe, and feel the way I do?

These are the kinds of questions I often ask myself. Having grown up in poverty, for reasons I don't quite understand, set me on a lifelong journey of asking questions. When things don't add up, I start asking questions. And while this has sometimes opened a can of worms, it has also helped me overcome the impossible. Other people with a similar background may say they're not successful because their family was poor, or they didn't have a father growing up. They have a list of excuses and justifications for their situation. They default to being the victim. But life is very short and we create our reality. Do we really have time for that kind of thinking?

CURIOUSLY CONTRARIAN

Like most people, I'm susceptible to external pressures, whether they're social pressures or stem from current economic conditions, politics, or public policies. We all get caught up in reacting to the latest fads, news cycles, and "clickbait" headlines. We hear or read "predictions" from the "experts" about the economy and wonder what should we do, who should we listen to, *what actually is truth*?

In general, TWF adopts a contrarian mindset that goes

against the crowd. Usually, we don't adopt popular thinking or do what everyone else does just because it's popular. The Wealth Builder prefers to dig deeper and come to his own conclusions.

Not everyone will want to undertake that kind of study and self-inquiry. Nor does everyone need to in order to become financially independent. While it's been important for me to think independently, search things out, and ask questions, you can simply choose to master the three pillars of Debt, Income, and Assets without delving into the esoteric. With this book, you'll learn everything you need to know in order to create financial freedom, even if you have no desire whatsoever to understand historical patterns or current trends. Having an understanding of human nature, however, is critical if you want to preserve and protect your hard-earned money.

MONEY VS. WEALTH

We often think that money and wealth are the same thing, but they aren't. Let's take a closer look.

There are a number of ways to define money. We might define money as a medium of exchange or a store of value. Some people believe that money is the root of all evil. Perhaps we think of a dollar bill, which is a piece of paper backed by the Federal Reserve System (though in actuality it's backed by taxpayers, and then ultimately by *trust*).

A dollar represents our faith in the United States Treasury. However, at some point in time, maybe in the future, our faith in the system will begin to unravel, just as it has throughout history whenever paper money isn't backed by tangible or hard assets. But that's another story. For now, let's say we generally think of money as cash, whether it's in our hands or in the bank.

The meaning of wealth, on the other hand, is often overlooked and not considered very deeply. We tend to think about wealth simplistically only in terms of material possessions.

If you want to build wealth and financial security, then it's important to consider what wealth means to you. Think about it for yourself: What does wealth mean to me? How do I define true wealth? What is my context for thinking about wealth?

I've thought about wealth for a long time, and have come up with a list of what I consider true wealth means.

TRUE WEALTH DEFINED

I define true wealth in several ways.

The first has to do with spirituality. In my case, I describe it as my personal relationship with the Creator. By that I don't mean my relationship with the Creator via another person or through organized religion. I'm referring to the quality and fruit of my spiritual life: my level of inner peace and fulfillment, how I treat others, and from whom and where I get my core identity and validation.

You may define the spiritual in another way. This is something that each one of us decides for ourselves. For me **spirit** is number one when it comes to defining what true wealth is.

Number two on my list is **health**. Someone may have all the money in the world, but if they're in poor health, they're not going to be able to enjoy their wealth.

Three has to do with **family and relationships**. I think everyone would agree that family and relationships are a part of true wealth. When people are on their deathbed, they generally don't say, I wish I made more money. Instead, they usually say they wish they spent more time with the people they love.

These two issues are interrelated. You might argue that relationships come before health, and I wouldn't disagree with that. Without good health, including mental health, a person is not going to have healthy relationships with others. Many relationships are dysfunctional because a person is going through a situation that is emotionally difficult. The root cause can often be traced back to unresolved wounds and spiritual issues.

Personal liberty and freedom are number four on my list. They are part of true wealth because if we don't have the freedom to take risks, like starting a new business, we won't be able to solve problems in the marketplace or create opportunity for ourselves and others.

We're fortunate to live in countries where we enjoy liberty and freedom of movement, thought, and expression, as well as access to information and self-education opportunities. Many people don't have the freedoms we take for granted. We have to be willing to protect our freedoms. The Founding Fathers, who wrote the US Constitution and Bill of Rights, discussed the delicate balance between freedom and security. We're in a time now where those key issues have come to the forefront once again. We should all remain vigilant because *freedom has a direct impact on our ability to create and experience true wealth.*

If you visit or study countries with totalitarian regimes, you clearly see the relationship between freedom and security: the less freedom there is, the less prosperity. America is not perfect, and it's certainly not the only country in the world that is prosperous. Many countries may be better than America in some ways, but it can be argued that no other country in history has fostered individual freedom, opportunity, and prosperity as has the United States. There is a direct correlation between the amount of freedom we have and the degree of our prosperity. I may have grown up poor, but I didn't grow up in a country without opportunity. And that has made all the difference.

Number five on my list is **financial independence and other resources**, though they may not have the same priority for you. You may place financial independence higher or lower on your list.

Having financial independence means we no longer have to work to earn money to pay the bills. As I mentioned earlier, my first wealth mentor Damien taught me: *the number one key to wealth is to get your money working for you instead of you working for your money*. This is a cornerstone statement of our TWF methodology, and we're going to continue to build on it.

Financial independence enables you to focus on what gives you the most purpose to your life, and it makes it possible to give back in ways you find the most meaningful. We've reached a point where, even if my wife, Dani, or I didn't work, we'd still be able to cover the basic needs of our family, thanks to the assets we have in place. It has enabled us to pursue a bigger purpose. We now live in the Wealth Builder quadrant and enjoy the TWF lifestyle of freedom, adventure, security, and fulfillment in our lives.

The degree of financial independence and the extent of other resources, such as contacts and quality relationships with people, have a direct impact on our freedom. They enable us to travel and live wherever we want, which is especially relevant now that we no longer need to live in a single geographical location in order to get work done. Today, *with the right set of skills, we can make money from almost anywhere in the world.*

Being free and fulfilled is more important to me than simply amassing money. Money can't guarantee my happiness. Religious people say you can't serve God and money at the same time. And while that's true, they have misunderstood the context. What that really means is that you have to establish priorities. You have to put your spiritual health, your relationship with the Creator and other people, ahead of money. You *can* do both. *You can have both monetary resources and spiritual peace and strength if you prioritize and invest your time accordingly.*

The next item on my list is **generational wealth and legacy**. This is part of living a life of meaning and fulfillment. Once our needs are taken care of, we're free to focus on our family legacy and what we can pass onto future generations. That includes not only money but also sharing our knowledge, experience, wisdom, insights, values, and the specialized skills we've learned in life.

Number eight is **meaningful accomplishments, purpose, and vision**. For me, true wealth includes a sense of discovery, fulfillment, and actualization of my life's purpose and vision. If I have all the material goods in the world but lack a sense of purpose and a meaningful vision in life, I'll become the Rich Miserable Bastard, and that sucks.

Last but not least is **contentment**, which I'm discovering more and more is the richness that comes from having a grateful heart. That's where true wealth really lies. We can make millions of dollars and achieve all kinds of goals, personal and financial, yet never feel like we have enough. Especially in Western society, which programs us to continually want and need more and more, we are never satisfied. Our culture tells us that more is better, that bigger is better. This is a lie. Contentment and gratitude are doorways to freedom, and they reveal a secret truth, that bigger isn't necessarily better and that maybe, just maybe...*less is more*. Contentment comes from having, or more accurately from *being* true wealth. *True wealth comes from the heart*. It is an inner wealth of living by the law of Love and from a full heart.

TREND AWARENESS

It's critical to look at both long- and short-term historical patterns, and to cultivate an awareness of current trends shaping our culture to get much-needed context.

A major trend today is the impact technology is having on literally everything. It's permeating all sectors of business and the economy, and it's a force multiplier. It's a lever: the input of new technology produces an output multiple times greater. In other words, things are changing quickly and drastically in our world thanks to technology, innovation, and disruption.

What went on in recent years in the oil-and-gas industry is a case in point. Oil and gas are commodities, natural resources like lumber or coffee. Like all commodities, the oil-and-gas industry goes through boom and bust cycles. It goes up or down depending on supply and demand.

Fracking and horizontal drilling are fairly new technological developments that have had an enormous impact on the industry and exploded supply, first in natural gas and then in oil. When OPEC (the Organization of the Petroleum Exporting Countries) lowered gas prices in 2015, they said that they were going to stop restricting supply. They would keep producing oil, which created a short-term trend of higher supply and lower oil prices. Even though OPEC's decision was an important trigger, it was really the underlying impact of technological innovation and years of fracking and horizontal drilling that caused the massive glut and excess capacity.

Technology is having a huge effect on medicine via biotech, on data storage and retrieval, and on hundreds of other industries. There's even a mobile app now, as one small example, that provides notary services, so you no longer have to go to the bank or pay a notary to get a document notarized. This is a phenomenon of disruptive technology or creative destruction. On one hand, a job is lost, and on the other, it places more power in the hands of people. Innovation brings a lot of beneficial change but at the same time disrupts the status quo.

Many of us used to think that technology would only impact a few things, but now we know it will have a much broader impact on the economy than we expected and will disrupt more jobs than ever imagined. Twenty years from now the world won't look the same. Self-driving vehicles, which were science fiction only a few years ago, will fill the roads.

Whether it's growth in the size of government or the development of artificial intelligence and robotics—what I call the Rise of the Machines—many of these trends are not going away, though it's hard to know exactly how they'll play out. The important thing is to keep an eye on the trajectory of current trends and also determine if they're repeating patterns from the past.

HISTORICAL PATTERNS

By studying history, we're able to see patterns and cycles that continually repeat themselves. Having an awareness of historical patterns helps you manage your resources, your views on politics and the proper role of government.

A little over forty years ago, the United States was the world's largest creditor nation. Today, we're the largest debtor nation in the world. In a mere forty years, our economy changed from one that was based on production to one based on debt and consumption.

The underlying problems of the 2008 global financial crisis continue today. The solution to too much debt was solved with more debt—remember the "too-big-to-fail" bailouts, monetary easing, etc.—which have only extended and prolonged the real problem.

Structurally, none of the deeper issues were dealt with. As history proves, ever-increasing debt is not sustainable. There's nothing new about expanding monetary supply. It's happened before throughout history, and it always ends the same way. Our overreliance on debt-fueled growth only makes our society more *fragile* during this time of great transition and instability. We have moved beyond the Industrial Age, blitzed through the Information Age, and are rapidly accelerating into the Machine Age. We are in *uncharted territory*, historically speaking, but we are repeating the very same patterns of human nature since the beginning of time. Indeed, there is nothing new under the sun.

Our country is on a path that every single democracy throughout history has followed. Democracies go through cycles of liberty, freedom, and self-reliance followed by cycles of apathy and dependency. Over time as people become more entitled, the public treasury begins to go bankrupt. Then, citizens look for a savior, a strong political figure to rescue them. This has happened throughout history in various ways. It often ends up in tyranny, less freedom, and more governmental control. Eventually over time through much travail and tragedy, things cycle back to spiritual liberation and self-reliance. The cycle of democracies continually repeats itself because *human nature fundamentally does not change.*

If you want to understand what's going on in the world today, become a student of history and learn to pay attention to trends and patterns. Then you'll understand where we are now, and how to best position yourself to survive and thrive in the chaos, instead of expecting someone else to solve your problems.

I'm not a historian, but I do ask questions. I believe we get the right answers when we ask the right questions.

THE CYCLE OF DEMOCRACY

Let's take a closer look at the life cycle of a democracy. It has been said that the average democracy lasts about 200 years. Throughout history, democracies progress through a sequence that goes roughly like this:

A nation starts out under bondage and tyranny. Living under persecution forces people to focus on developing spiritual strength because they have nothing else. They're oppressed, abused, and brutalized. The boot is on their neck, so they develop spiritual faith as a response to living under bondage.

Having spiritual faith, people develop courage. You can see this in the founding of America. The original patriots were courageous. Out of their bravery came liberty and freedom from British oppression.

With liberty, a democracy moves into abundance and prosperity. *Liberty and freedom create abundance and prosperity, not the other way around.* Prosperity does not arise from entitlement, handouts, or someone making the world perfect and safe for you.

In America's case, the Founding Fathers warned us to be careful about sacrificing our freedom for security. You can't have it both ways. Today Americans and many Western democracies want security, but I believe it's more important to maintain a balance between the two. If not, we risk losing our rights and privacy for the sake of a false illusion of security.

The next stage in the life cycle of a democracy goes from abundance to selfishness. After selfishness comes complacency and apathy. Apathy leads to dependency, which always ends in fiscal collapse due to voters voting themselves benefits from the public treasury. Eventually, a "strong man" leader is elected to "solve the problem," often leading to wars with a focus on an external enemy (real or created), tyranny, and oppression. Then it's back to bondage and tyranny, and the cycle starts all over again.

Where is the United States today? We've become a soft, selfish people, even though we still have significant abundance. And many Americans have become apathetic and complacent. What's most concerning is the growth of dependency, with some studies showing that close to half of the US population is now paying zero net income tax or dependent on benefits.

Democracy, or majority rule, cannot remain a stable form of government. It lasts only until the time when citizens realize they can vote themselves more public assistance, which puts more strain on the national treasury. From then on, those candidates who promise citizens more benefits are elected, and democracy starts to erode. Eventually, it collapses due to loose fiscal policy, which creates a ripe opportunity for dictatorship. A strong man or woman who promises to fix the problem appears on the scene. Fundamentally, the concept of democracy is only sustainable with a well-informed and educated population united by a common value system.

Our country was founded as a Republic, not a Democracy. The word "democracy" is not in the US Constitution, not in the Declaration of Independence, and not in the Bill of Rights. In a Republic, *the rights of the minority are protected from the majority*. In a Democracy, two wolves and a sheep vote on what's for dinner. Majority rule sounds fair, but it can be a terrible and wicked thing, and because of conformity and groupthink, it is also easily manipulated.

MINDSET

A critical part of TWF is understanding what makes us tick personally. What are my strengths and weaknesses mentally, psychologically, and emotionally? What are my ideas about money and wealth, and where did they come from? The more we know about ourselves, the stronger our wealth-building structure will be.

Human beings are irrational. We think we make decisions logically, but the truth is we rarely do. We may sit down and come up with a set of plans and follow through on them for a while, but when something changes that affects us emotionally, we set our plans aside and resort to our feelings.

I had a young friend who was methodically building up his bank account and focused on financial stability. Then he met the girl of his dreams. All of a sudden, he started spending all his hard-earned money. His priorities changed. Why? Because his heart was affected. His emotions became involved, and his very rational and logical savings plan went out the window!

Another example is our response to the stock market. As I write this book, we're in one of the longest bull markets in history. But it's also been called the most hated bull market because so many people were burned in the last two market corrections—the dot-com bubble that burst in 2000 and the global financial crisis of 2008. Many people are sitting on the sidelines and have missed this boom cycle. Typically, the way these markets end is that at the last minute, the masses jump in, excited at the prospect of making easy money, and rather than enjoying the ride up, they end up riding the market down again because they have no strategy and no exit plan.

We all know cognitively we should buy low and sell high,

but statistically that's not what most people do. Instead, we follow the herd. We fall under the influence of our friends and peers. We end up buying or selling at the wrong time. And we do that because we don't have a strategy or a plan. We don't invest. We gamble. "Buy and hold" becomes buy and fold. We buy high and sell low, then repeat until we're broke. We know what we're supposed to do, but we don't do it. Why? Human nature. As an entrepreneur and marketer, I learned early on that people buy on emotion and then rationalize their purchase with facts. We are, at our core, emotional buyers and sellers.

There are other ways our mindset affects our capacity to acquire wealth. Memorize this truth and TWF law: *no one will do for you what you are not willing to do for yourself.* No one is going to pay attention to your money like you will. You care more about your money than a money manager or a professional investor ever will. They may have more knowledge and experience than you, but they won't care as much.

How many people put time and effort into educating themselves sufficiently to manage their money successfully? We prefer to defer to someone who'll tell us what to do. We're unwilling to take responsibility for our decisions and actions, which I can tell you firsthand is dangerous when it comes to money, finances, and wealth-building.

True Wealth Formula encourages you to think for yourself. Begin by being willing to ask questions. Don't simply sit down and shut up like we were taught to do in school, and don't feel ridiculed for asking a stupid question. We're conditioned to conform and consume, but to succeed we need to do the opposite.

Start by embracing the journey of self-discovery and examine the influences and beliefs that drive your decisions. Have you heard or believed any of these common success myths?

- Fake it until you make it.
- Don't show any vulnerability.
- Show your success.
- Build it once and it'll last forever.
- Be willing to do whatever it takes to succeed.
- Never quit, no matter what.

These and other beliefs may be deeper in your thinking than you realize. And they can have devastating effects on your wealth-building when applied without wisdom in the wrong place and time.

NATURAL LAWS AND KNOWLEDGE OF THE CREATOR

In addition to paying attention to your mindset and

unconscious behaviors, studying historical patterns, and observing current trends, it's also critical to have an understanding of natural or spiritual laws when building true wealth. I like to refer to those fundamental principles as the laws of the Creator. They are basic spiritual principles that never change, and they are the essentials of living a good life.

We've all heard the Golden Rule: *treat people the way you want to be treated*. Even if we know we can't go around screwing people over, we're often quick to rationalize or justify our less-than-noble behaviors. We prefer to blame the other person. We defend treating a customer poorly by saying he was rude. But when it's time for the boss to make a promotion, he's not going to choose the employee who's habitually unkind to customers, no matter how talented he or she may be. That's how the natural Law of Stewardship and being faithful in the small things play out in life.

The Law of Stewardship says that he who is trusted with little will be made ruler over much. That means if you're faithful in the small things, like treating your customers well, opportunities will open up for you, and you'll be given authority over more. The law applies to our finances and investing too.

Spiritual principles affect our relationships with other

people and ourselves, and they influence how we deal with money and resources. Whether you believe in these laws or not, they are natural forces at work in the world.

GOALS OF TRUE WEALTH FORMULA

True Wealth Formula is a system for building financial independence which consists of a solid Foundation, the three pillars of Debt, Income, and Assets, and our Legacy. It's a way of living that goes beyond the amount of money you have in your bank account or the number of material goods you possess.

What are your reasons for achieving financial independence? Goals for True Wealth Formula that I've identified are tied to personal liberty, which I believe is the number one reason for seeking financial independence. This includes being able to:

- come and go as we please
- spend time with the people we want to be with
- engage in work that we enjoy, fulfills us, makes a contribution, and gives meaning to our life
- give back, whether to members of our family, to society, or in any other way that is important to us

Personal liberty means having freedom of movement and being able to travel. We've gained an incredible education by visiting over forty countries, meeting other people, learning about foreign cultures, and discovering different histories and value systems that underlie economics.

Personal liberty includes freedom of thinking and speaking our mind without fear of reprisal. It includes the freedom to associate with people who share our values and the freedom to educate ourselves. Privacy is a freedom, which regrettably is eroding today at an alarming rate. Personal liberty also includes freedom of conscientious objection, the ability to disagree with the status quo, and not being forced to do something we don't believe in. Having financial independence enables us to enjoy all of these freedoms.

PORTABLE INCOME SOURCES

Being able to generate a portable income means you're not constrained by geography in order to earn a living. Because your money is working for you, you can be located anywhere in the world. Technology and changes in telecommunications have helped make this a reality. If you want to pick up your family and live in another part of the country or world, you can. You have the freedom to choose your lifestyle.

Investors, too, can explore geographically and politically diversified assets. Now there are numerous opportunities for making investments in foreign markets and you can manage a portfolio from anywhere in the world from a mobile app. You no longer have to restrict investments to where you live.

WORKS FOR EVERYONE

True Wealth Formula, as you'll learn, works for everyone, including the typical hard-working average guy. It's not a system that's for high earners or rich people only. It's a method and a mindset that anyone can adopt to improve his or her life, achieve financial independence, and create a wealth-building machine.

True Wealth Formula isn't dependent on how much money a person has. Rather, it provides a system for being a good steward of any amount of money you possess and learning how to make it grow and compound. It's based on sound principles that provide methods and rules anyone can implement. It's evergreen and crosses all socioeconomic and educational distinctions.

HONORS PEOPLE AND THE CREATOR

True Wealth Formula is not a system for getting rich at the expense of other people, whether through mismanagement of shared natural resources on the planet or by bringing harm to others.

CHARACTERISTICS OF TRUE WEALTH FORMULA

A number of specific characteristics of TWF make it a unique system for building wealth and financial independence.

First, TWF is characterized by **defensive thinking**. Defensive thinking asks, "What if?" What if the investment I'm making ends up failing? If it fails, how will I feel? Who am I trusting? What if things don't turn out? What if I'm wrong? These are typical defensive-type questions that lie at the center of our approach.

Another characteristic of TWF is **to be strategic**. Tactics take advantage of opportunities that present themselves in the moment: that sounds like a good idea; let's try it. Tactics have their function, but understanding how opportunities fit into a larger long-term strategy is more important. To be strategic means having an overall game plan or rules by which to play in order to win.

Patience is an attribute of the TWF approach. It can be hard to be patient, and it often goes against our nature (for some of us more than others), but having patience plays a big role in making good decisions.

Resiliency characterizes the TWF and means sticking to a strategy. Of course, mistakes will sometimes be made, and failures can and will happen, but when they do—when we get beaten, bruised, kicked, and knocked on our butts—we make sure we learn everything we possibly can from the experience. *We extract maximum educational value out of every mistake and failure, and we make the mistake our slave forever from that point forward.* No one can go through life without making mistakes, but each of us can control our attitude towards them and how we'll respond.

True Wealth Formula is **systematic.** It's methodical. We aim to follow a strategy and proceed step by step.

Whenever possible, TWF operates on **autopilot.** Wherever we can, we find ways to automate **non-discretionary** systems, money-management principles, and investment strategies because *we value simplicity in our lives.* We value simplicity more than money and don't want to be its slave. Rather, we want money to be our slave, so we automate processes with the use of technology and other mechanisms.

Non-discretionary means not subject to or influenced by someone's discretion, judgment, or preference. In other words, once the rules are set up, they are followed. They are not changed because of how we feel in the moment.

Building momentum is a characteristic of TWF and includes both psychological and financial momentum.

When we see progress being made, we become encouraged, and things begin to take on a life of their own.

Diversity characterizes the True Wealth Formula. We strive to make sure that our investments are diversified. We never want to be in a position where we risk a catastrophic loss from a single event or mistake. Whether on our balance sheet, in our asset base, or in our portfolio of stocks, bonds, real estate, or other assets, we take care not to expose ourselves to catastrophic loss.

TWF focuses on **allocation**. We pay attention to asset allocations and specifically to asset-characteristic allocations.

Another characteristic is **liquidity**. We want to understand the difference between liquid and illiquid assets. We don't want to find ourselves in the position of being "land rich but cash poor" or getting caught on the wrong side of a "liquidity squeeze" in the next market crash.

TWF values **adaptability**. We adapt our thinking and investment strategies according to market conditions, the environment, and current trends. We don't expect the market, or other people for that matter, to conform to us.

We like **portability**. We ask how relocation would affect our wealth strategy and our ability to manage our asset base. Does it tie us down to a single location?

We like **tangibility** and don't want to overlook the value of hard assets because all wealth ultimately comes from the earth. Hard assets include everything from precious metals, like silver, gold, and platinum, to gas, oil, productive farmland, rental real estate, or other assets that have intrinsic value.

Time-tested is a quality of the True Wealth Formula. We look at long spans of time, and at historical cycles and patterns to learn what has stood the test of time. We prefer evergreen strategies, staying power, and timeless principles, but we'll seize on good short-term speculations when the opportunity arises.

TWF favors **production** overconsumption. Creating value lies in producing more than you consume.

We are highly biased towards **cash-flow assets**. We make a clear distinction between investing and speculating and give you simple rules and allocations to follow to build and compound assets that make you richer every year instead of poorer.

And lastly, True Wealth Formula is **politically atheistic**. We don't place our hopes on any one political orientation. We don't believe in staking our financial future, for ourselves and for our family, on politics. However, we do acknowledge that political trends have a serious impact on our wealth-building efforts and financial freedom and are not to be ignored.

CHAPTER 3

DEBT

DEALING WITH THE ROOT

Before we can get into the meat of "how to get our money working for us instead of us working for our money," we've got some issues to address.

A key characteristic of the Wealth Builder is that he's on the production side of the economy instead of the consumption side. This is why, in TWF, the first of our three pillars to master is the Debt pillar. It is also where we begin learning how to *be faithful in the small things, so that we can be made ruler over much.*

Many people believe that if they could just make more money, their financial problems would be over. If they can't pay their bills on time or don't like their lifestyle, they think increasing their income is the best and only solution. It's a popular mindset and a social program that results in too many people spending their lives focused only on how to make more money.

That mindset leads down the path of working to perform better at a job, searching for another career, starting a new business, or going back to school. Your income may go up if you do those things, but you'll continue with the same habits that got you into debt in the first place: you'll start spending more money as soon as you have more.

You have to attack the problem at its root, at the level of your beliefs and mindset. Our core behavior is driven by subconscious programs and motivations. It just makes sense that, if we increase our income, we should be able to spend more. We move into a better neighborhood, take a more extravagant vacation, eat at fancier restaurants, wear designer clothes, or join a more prestigious club. This cycle continues the habit of overspending and living beyond our means. In almost every case, making more money just means having bigger debts.

If your goal is to build true wealth and financial independence so that you have freedom, security, and fulfillment (the life of the Wealth Builder), then *you have to deal with the root cause of debt*: your mindset and the absence of having a proven system in place to manage your money.

IN DEBT WE TRUST

Our global economy is a debt-driven economy. As mentioned earlier, forty years ago the United States was the world's largest creditor nation and today is the world's largest debtor nation. When the dollar went off the gold standard in 1971, the checks and balances on how the economy expands and grows were removed. This led to the situation we're in now, in which, for the economy to keep growing, debt levels have to keep rising. This is unsustainable, and it will not end well. The "powers that be" (global banks, corporations, and governments) have a vested interest in your continued addiction to consumerism, as they are the primary benefactors.

Unfortunately, our own human nature and impatience are to blame: Why should I wait until I have the money to pay for what I want when *I can afford the payments*? Why delay gratification? Why save money when I can have what I want now? There's no fun in that!

This mindset sets in from the time we're very young. We're programmed and conditioned to be consumers and go into debt. We're told to go to school and then get a job. We go to college to get a good education, which for most requires going into debt, at which time we receive our first credit card offers. We graduate with the equivalent of a mortgage to pay off, but without the house. Jobs aren't there in our chosen degree or field, and we have no real assets backing our debt-based education.

Corporations spend billions of dollars on advertising to get you to spend money. The media constantly feeds our belief that we need to purchase something in order to be valued, feel good about ourselves, or to fill a void in our lives. We're bombarded 24/7 by messages that condition us to be good little consumers. The government even tells us during recessions that spending is a form of patriotism—do your part and go shopping!

There's nothing new about this. We're going through a cycle that has repeated itself many times throughout history. Money inflates and eventually becomes devalued. Low interest rates and debt-fueled overconsumption accelerate the process. The more prosperous a society becomes, the more indulgent it is, and the lazier people become. We get fat and entitled, and we rationalize our softness.

Again, in a debt-based economy like ours, debt must continue to increase in order for the economy to expand and grow. The only way this will change is if one of two things happens: either there is a radical and fundamental change in what drives the economy, or the economy or government hits a point at which it can no longer continue servicing the ever-increasing debt load.

The best thing you can do in this situation is take personal responsibility and cease to be a victim of debt and consumption. This book will help you. It provides all the tools and understanding you need to take control and become free in today's economy, or in any phase of the economic cycle. But you have to get serious about it and stop rationalizing your debt and financial situation. There is an old proverb: the borrower is servant to the lender. In other words, *debt is slavery*. You may not want to hear that, but it's true. *You were not created to be a slave. You were created to take dominion as a wise steward and manager over your territory and resources.*

The world is changing rapidly. We're fully engulfed in the Information Age, and, as I stated previously, we've already entered the Machine Age of artificial intelligence (AI) and robotics. The economic model that people have relied on for decades is fading, and it won't come back. Universal income (welfare) won't fix things either, as that brings a whole host of other, much deeper problems. Decentralized cryptocurrencies are promising and disruptive but still very early and unproven technologies. Our moment in history requires a new way of thinking about money and the cultivation of new habits if we want to experience financial independence and live the life of the Wealth Builder.

Debt has become a socially acceptable habit and way of

life. Most people acquire debt before they have an income to support it. Worse, there is no understanding of the difference between bad debt and "good" debt. That's why TWF begins with the Debt pillar. It shows you how to take the prison of negative compound interest on which the payment of debt is based and turn it on its head into a wealth-building machine.

THE MONEY QUADRANT

Now before we continue with the Debt pillar and our journey of mastery over our money, I want to introduce you to a simple and incredibly powerful concept in TWF called The Money Quadrant. If you memorize the chart I'm going to show you, it will forever change how you view, spend, and invest your money, and how you perceive the physical world around you.

There are four types of debts and assets on a *balance sheet.*

WHAT'S A BALANCE SHEET?

A balance sheet is a list of your assets and liabilities. The difference between the value of the two is your net worth. If you have more assets than liabilities, you have a positive net worth. If you have more liabilities than assets, you have a negative net worth.

Everyone has a balance sheet whether they are aware of it or not. We'll be talking more about the balance sheet and how it impacts wealth-building and financial freedom.

Now let's continue.

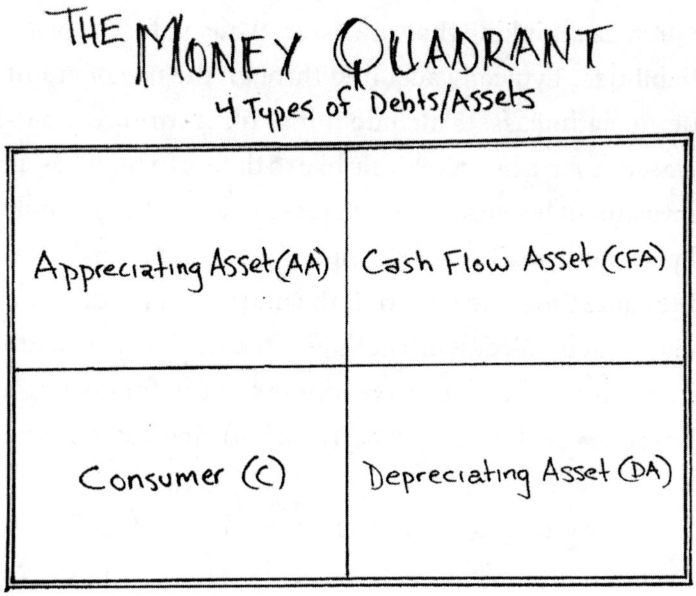

In the bottom left corner of the Money Quadrant lies **Consumer Debt**, which is the type of debt credit cards enable. There is nothing on the balance sheet (no assets) to offset the debt (liability), because the money has been spent or consumed, whether on food, medical bills, or travel. Moreover, your monthly credit card payments include the compounded interest on your consumption at an average rate of 17% to 22% or higher. *Consumer debt is the worst type of debt there is.*

On the bottom right of the quadrant are **Depreciating Assets.** They are the most common type of debt for the middle class. Depreciating assets are items people purchase, thinking they are assets while in fact they are liabilities. Typically acquired through the use of credit, depreciating assets include things like furniture, boats, cars, or even a house. People like to think of a house as an investment because it *may* increase in value, but you only build equity in a house over time *if* the market is rising. At the same time, the materials the house is made of depreciate and break down. That's why the IRS lets you take a depreciation deduction on your tax return for owning a house or commercial property that is a dedicated rental.

The moment you drive a new car off the lot, you start losing money. Vehicles have the highest rate of depreciation during the first three years after their purchase. It's much smarter to never buy a new vehicle and only purchase cars that are at least three years old. Then you minimize the depreciation factor.

One of the worst things you can do if you're serious about becoming wealthy is to buy a car with a loan. Why do so many people do it all the time? Because a car makes people feel good. Advertising conditions us to buy a new car, to consume, and to go into debt. We feel pressure from our peers and want to keep up with the Joneses. We like to present a certain public image, and we need the reinforcement of a nice vehicle to make us feel good about ourselves. All those things contribute to why we go into debt to buy a new car. If you need a car, pay cash. If you have the discretionary income to buy a boat, then don't finance it.

Everyone will have some amount of depreciating assets on their balance sheet. What you have to remember is to *never incur debt to finance a depreciating asset*. One of the keys to creating wealth is to eliminate depreciating asset debt from your balance sheet.

On the top left of the Money Quadrant diagram is **Appreciating Assets**, which are assets that have the *potential* to increase in value over time.

An example of an appreciating asset is land. Land may go up or it may go down in value over time, *depending on market cycles*. A piece of artwork, rare coins, and other collectibles could also be considered appreciating assets. Quality artwork, if you buy smart, tends to go up in value over time. Financing the purchase of a business could be an appreciating asset. Starting a new business (a startup) is an appreciating asset, until it becomes established and is consistently generating positive cash flow.

The key thing to remember about appreciating assets is that they should not be acquired through debt whenever possible. *They are speculative assets.* They're exciting, but you have zero control over whether they'll increase in value or not. That means *you must get the timing right, which very few people consistently do.* Appreciating assets, like depreciating assets, almost always produce a negative cash flow, which I'll explain next.

The fourth type of asset, in the upper right quadrant of the chart, is a **Cash-Flow Asset.**

If there is such a thing as "good debt," a cash-flow asset would be it. It's what the wealthy use to increase their wealth, though they do so conservatively and strategically. They never leverage more than the underlying asset is worth, and they make sure the asset is cash-flow positive.

A great example of a cash-flow asset is a rental house. One of our sons owns a rental property. It was a foreclosure he bought with money he had saved for a down payment. He secured financing for the balance and had repairs done to the house. Now the property yields positive cash flow of $417 per month. The rental property pays him more money than the total of all his expenses, including the mortgage, interest, and insurance costs. He did this at the age of fifteen.

If our son decides he no longer wants to rent the house and to live in it instead, the property would technically no longer be a cash-flow asset. It would become a depreciating asset, with the *potential* for appreciation only if and when it is sold at a profit and realizes a capital gain *after all expenses are paid*.

Other examples of a positive cash-flow asset include dividend-paying stocks, municipal bonds, and private notes or loans secured by a first deed of trust or an established business, as long as it consistently earns profits after all expenses, such as salaries, are paid. Used wisely and smartly like the wealthy do, a cash-flow asset can increase wealth and grow your asset base through both positive cash flow *and* appreciation.

HOW TO TURN A LIABILITY INTO AN ASSET

The dad of my best friend Chris from Hawaii always kept an old car sitting in his driveway. He drove the car for years. It was an old "jalopy," with the keys always in the ignition. All of his neighbors and friends knew that if they ever needed a car for the day, they could take his as long as they brought it back with a new quart of oil, as it always leaked.

One day I went up to Chris's dad and asked, "Steve, you have plenty of money. Why don't you buy a new car?"

He replied, "I take the money I'd be using to make payments on a new car and put it in my retirement account instead."

I walked away from that exchange and thought he was brilliant. I thought to myself, so that's how you turn a liability into an investment. I have never forgotten that principle, and it is core TWF thinking and strategy.

Chris's dad and many others continued driving that car for many years after we talked. In fact, my wife, Dani, and I borrowed that car on our honeymoon to save money!

HOW TO LOSE EVERYTHING

In summary, three of the four types of debt are bad forms of debt and wealth-killers. The two types of debt on the bottom of the chart, consumer debt and depreciating asset debt, are *absolute no-go red zones.*

The top-left quadrant, appreciating asset debt, is a yellow zone and requires *extreme* caution. For most people, these types of assets end up being little more than speculations, though many investors end up using debt as leverage to speculate. The stock and real estate markets prove the point. When the market goes up, people take out loans (or trade on margin), believing they'll catch the ride and will never lose money. They take out a second mortgage or secure a loan that exceeds the value of their house, thinking they'll sell the speculative house in a year and make a profit. They justify the excessive loan-to-value ratios, convinced they'll make a lot of money in the rising market. These appreciating-asset, speculative-debt bubble activities are, for most people, simply a form of gambling.

You may be successful with a first house and even a second or a third one. *The problems begin with success, not failure.* When you're having success, you start leveraging up, which everyone does in a rising market because it's only natural to do more of what's working. With increasing leverage and growing debt, you can get caught on the wrong side of the market cycle, and suddenly, with only a single loss, everything gets wiped out like dominoes. This is how people blow up their accounts (in trading terms) or otherwise implode their balance sheets. They are *over-leveraged* and don't have the *situational awareness* or a system to anticipate and manage risk when the market rolls over. TWF will give you the system and investing rules to follow so this never happens to you.

A couple I know made several million dollars in real estate, only to lose it all by sinking everything into a "can't lose" speculative development project. The market began to turn, then rolled over and crashed. All their money was tied up in an *illiquid speculative* project that went bust. The game was over, and they were totally wiped out. When you have an experience like that, it affects you psychologically and messes with your head. My friends never recovered.

Unless you are a professional speculator with a solid long-term track record, you need to exercise *extreme caution* when dealing with appreciating asset debt. For the vast majority of people without specific skill and insider knowledge in land speculation, commodities, real estate, the stock market, or trading in other types of appreciating assets, *it's best to have no appreciating asset debt*, which I'll discuss when I explain TWF money management and investing ratios later in the book.

Another overlooked consequence of these types of speculations is they are almost always negative-cash-flow assets on your balance sheet. *The expenses associated with maintaining the asset will eat away at your bottom line, making you poorer every year, not richer.*

HOW THE WEALTHY BUDGET

Now I'm going to let you in on a secret of how the rich and ultra-wealthy manage their money. It's so simple, yet so powerful. When you learn and master it, you will never consider using boring, ineffective, traditional budgeting methods again. And *you will never again experience another year in which you aren't growing richer.*

In the TWF money management system, we don't use conventional budgeting methods taught by most accountants and financial advisors for one simple reason: they don't work.

The reason why they don't work is human nature. Most people don't actually follow conventional budgeting methods consistently. Remember, your subconscious is literally an 800-pound gorilla. You are not going to win so why fight it? Perhaps only one or two percent of the population has the personality and temperament to follow through on a conventional budget. Many people set up a budget and don't stick to it because they don't have a simple, automated system in place for maintaining it, or an emotional event arises, and the irrational mind takes over and does what it's been programmed to do...spend.

The dirty little secret is that you've been taught to budget and manage money the wrong way. *Wealthy people don't manage money based on dollars and cents. They focus on ratios.* In TWF we do what the wealthy do. We use ratio-based systems for managing our money and allocating investment capital.

PARKINSON'S LAW

Parkinson's law states that work expands to fill the time available for its completion. In other words, people use the full amount of time allocated for completing a task, no matter how much or how little time they set aside. For example, if I have to mow the lawn and give myself until the following weekend to do it, I won't get the lawn mown before the weekend. I'll wait until Saturday or Sunday to mow. However, if I'd wanted the lawn mown within thirty minutes, I'd have figured out the fastest, most efficient way to do it in the short amount of time I had.

Most people think Parkinson's law only applies to productivity and time management, but it applies to money management and wealth-building, too.

Memorize this TWF law: *money is always looking for a place to go.*

It will always be spent and consumed to fill whatever void is available to it. *If we don't tell our money where to go and what to do, what its purpose and reason for existence is, money will, in effect, tell us what to do.* Money will influence us. That may sound strange because, obviously, money doesn't talk and can't really tell us what to do. But the larger truth is we're conditioned and programmed to do one thing and one thing only with our money...to be a good consumer and spend!

If we're going to become *master* over our money, if we're going to make money our *slave* and get it working for us instead of us working for it, *we must tell our money what its purpose is, what its reason for existence is.* We do that through the system I'm going to show you right now.

HOW TO FIGHT A GORILLA

In TWF, we counter our social programming and conditioning by setting up *non-discretionary, rules-based systems* for our money. We implement default programs for allocating our money in ways that automatically move us toward our goals of wealth-building and freedom. We put into place money-management and investing systems that are *non-negotiable* and that are not dependent on our emotions or how we feel.

Our non-discretionary rules-based filters and systems give our money a purpose and a reason for existing. It tells money where to go and what to do, and it checkmates the 800-pound gorilla of our subconscious mind. It's a fundamental principle of the TWF system, and *it is the first step in becoming master over our money and making money our slave.*

NON-DISCRETIONARY RULE #1 (ND1)

So how do we implement this system? We apply the

10-10-10-70 Rule to every dollar we earn, whether the money comes from a paycheck, a gift, a bonus, or other windfall profit. *Every dollar we deposit is subject to this rule.*

The 10-10-10-70 Rule or ND1 is how we manage our *earned income* (the money we work for) and it works as follows:

- the first 10% of our money is set aside for Giving
- the second 10% goes into our Wealth account
- the third 10% is a Debt accelerator that goes towards debt repayment
- the remaining 70% is for our Bills, the money we use for daily living and related expenses

In TWF, we use this simple but powerful formula to overcome and deliver a knockout blow to the biggest liability to achieving wealth...ourselves and our very human emotions.

BE A GIVER: THE FIRST 10%

Why does TWF begin with the first 10% of our income going towards giving?

The answer lies in a universal spiritual law. If we are givers, according to this principle, we will be blessed with more. Another way to say this is that we reap what we sow. To be a giver means that you trust the Creator to provide, even if you have little. Giving activates the Law of Stewardship: because you are being faithful in the small things you've been entrusted with, you'll be given authority over bigger things.

To illustrate, consider a person who works in sales. If they don't sell, they don't eat. When things don't go well, they become stressed because they're not earning enough money from commissions to cover their bills. When that happens, they communicate non-verbally—it's claimed that ninety-three percent of all communication is non-verbal—that things are desperate for them, regardless of whatever they may say to the contrary. Human nature dictates that people are not attracted to a person whose non-verbal communication is neediness and desperation. A downward cycle sets in, and things get worse.

The way to reverse this downward spiral is to become a giver. Once you realize that you have all that you need and so much to be thankful for, you'll discover there are options. You'll begin to make adjustments to your life, like downsizing. And, first and foremost, you'll start giving.

Giving is a form of trust in the Creator and in His provision for your life. This spiritual law is closely connected to the Law of Stewardship. In addition to being a success law in business, finance, and wealth, *giving is one of the key antidotes to being a Rich Miserable Bastard.*

In business (or in any relationship), if I desperately want or need a person to buy or do something for me, they'll sense it. A needy person never gives. If I give instead, things will change on the spiritual level. I will be setting into motion principles that generate abundance and reciprocation in my life, and my non-verbal communication will change. Doors will open, and blessings will enter my life. The number of my contracts will increase, and sales will go up. Unexpected opportunities will present themselves, all because I obediently put into practice the spiritual principle of giving.

TWF doesn't stipulate where to give because that's a personal choice, but it does recommend giving according to where your passion lies. My wife, Dani, and I have given millions to orphanages, abused single moms, and children who truly need help. We like to give in a way that helps people help themselves. We don't like handouts because we think they create dependency. Rather than give a man a fish, we use our resources to teach him how to fish. And we don't believe in giving to support salaries and building programs. We want at least ninety percent of our donated money to go directly towards the recipient and not get lost in administrative expenses and overheads. Wherever or however you choose to give, be sure it lines up with your personal convictions and values.

Wealth Builders are givers, and giving is a large part of experiencing fulfillment in life. We give because it's a blessing to be able to give. We never know when we might be the person who needs to receive, and more importantly giving sets into motion positive outcomes.

PAY YOURSELF FIRST: THE SECOND 10%

The second 10% of your income goes towards a very powerful wealth principle: *pay yourself first*.

Many people have heard of this principle, but few actually implement it. That's because they lack a strategic and automated method for consistently applying the principle to every deposit, every week, every month, and every year.

TWF solves this dilemma with our non-discretionary rules-based 10-10-10-70 formula by putting the second 10% into your Wealth account, as I'll soon describe in more detail.

THE DEBT ACCELERATOR: THE THIRD 10%

The third 10% goes towards eliminating debt. We call it the Debt Accelerator payment.

The technicalities of how the debt accelerator payment works are fully explained later in this section.

LIVE WITHIN YOUR MEANS: THE 70% RULE

At its most fundamental level, wealth-building requires mastering the core habits of producing more than you consume (i.e., living below your means), and saving and investing the difference.

Our human nature tries to shortcut this process by chasing fantasies (the grass is greener syndrome), get rich quick schemes, entitlement (the victim identity), gambling, and using debt and other forms of speculation.

At its very core, living below your means is part of the Law of Stewardship key to true wealth. You might get lucky for a little while and feel like you're the exception and able to cheat this law, but that's an illusion.

If you're living in debt and overconsuming, then you are overspending and living above your means and thereby breaking that law. In TWF, we reverse this habit by following the 70% Rule of living off of 70% of our *earned income* (the money you work for).

Many people, when they hear they should live on seventy percent of their income, react by saying that they can barely live off of 100% now. But after implementing TWF, they discover they have a lot of unnecessary spending in their lives.

We tend to think that there are things we can't live without only to discover it wasn't true. Often, habits have developed that need to be done away with. My wife, Dani, through her War on Debt program, is the absolute best at helping people to "cut the fat" and identify excess spending from their budgets. In the end, it's a mental game and takes an aggressive no-holds-barred focus to deprogram years of social conditioning to spend and consume. If there's a shortcut, the TWF ND1 money management system is it.

LESS IS MORE

If reaching financial independence and having freedom, security, and fulfillment are a priority for you, you'll have to make some tough decisions. The crazy thing is, *doing so is actually a freeing experience.* You'll recognize that you didn't really need all the things you thought you did. Everything you thought was making you happy, all the consumption, wasn't bringing you any closer to the happiness you were truly seeking.

Many people find that even when they make more money, buy nice things, and have more stuff, they still feel like it's never enough, no matter the size of their bonus check, how successful their business has become, or how nice their house. It's never enough, and they want more. This is the life of the Rich Miserable Bastard. I've lived here. It sucks and it's no fun, believe me!

In our "bigger is better" culture, it can be a difficult thing to go against the grain. *We are literally baptized into the religion of consumerism, consumption, and debt*. We live in a super-sized culture. The question to ask yourself is: *is my stuff really making me any happier*?

In most Western societies today, *there seems to be a correlation between more and misery*. We become less happy the more we have. We become the Rich Miserable Bastard. *More is not better. Bigger is not better. Less is actually more.*

There's only one way to escape the prison of constantly seeking more, and that is to adopt an *offensive mindset*, to attack what is attacking us and do the exact opposite. The Wealth Builder and TWF practitioner are both fueled and empowered by a *minimalist* mindset. *Less isn't less. Less is freedom.*

Living on seventy percent goes back to the spiritual Law of Stewardship principle of being faithful in the small things. If we're not faithful with the money that we currently have, what makes us think that we'll be good stewards of our resources when we get a promotion, a raise, a better job, or our business doubles? It won't happen. The habits that we have today are the habits we'll have in the future.

But if we become good stewards and managers of the resources we currently have, no matter how small, we set up a *chain reaction* for other good things to come into our lives.

You have to be willing to step back and find out what it is you truly need. You have to take a hard look at your spending and get it down to seventy percent.

As long as you're living within seventy percent of your income, you are free to do whatever you want with your money. If you want an elaborate lifestyle, then go for it and don't feel bad about it because you're stewarding and managing your resources well.

Once you've mastered the three TWF pillars of Debt, Income, and Assets, you'll find that your income will begin to increase dramatically as will your asset base. Then you'll find yourself living off even less than seventy percent of your income.

HOW TO IMPLEMENT ND1: THE SPECIFICS

Implementing our ND1 10-10-10-70 Rule begins by setting up *four individual accounts*, which give your money a place to go. Remember, if you don't tell your money where to go, it will tell you. To become its master, you need to assign a specific purpose to your money.

How much money goes into each account is based on the 10-10-10-70 percentages. Not all of your money goes into a single account the way most people do it. Putting all your money into one account comingles funds that have different purposes. In TWF, we segregate our money and give it a reason for existence. We tell our money what its purpose is, and we are its master, not the other way around. The simplest and most effective way to do that is with separate accounts.

The first account and first 10% is the **Giving account**. In most cases, this will be a checking account.

The second account is the **Wealth account**. It receives the 10% of your income that you set aside to pay yourself. It could be a savings account at your local bank or a brokerage account, but it shouldn't be a typical savings account. The money in the Wealth account is NOT money you set aside for a rainy day or an "I can spend it when I need it" emergency fund.

The money in the Wealth account has a specific purpose. *Money is seed. We can either eat our seed or plant it.* If we plant our seed, there's the opportunity for it to grow into an orchard. Eventually, the orchard will produce fruit. We want to keep planting our seed and cultivating the orchard so that at some point in the future, we'll be able to walk into the orchard, pick the fruit, eat it, and enjoy it without it having any effect on the orchard. The orchard will keep producing fruit year after year. The potential lies in the seed, but if we eat the seed, we'll never get the orchard.

Again, and this point is critical, *our Wealth account money is our seed money*. It is not a "savings account" for taking withdrawals; *it is for planting*. The Wealth account begins as a single account, but over time evolves into an estate structure that can include multiple accounts, properties, businesses, Limited Liability Companies (LLCs), Corporations, and other types of entities. In general terms, "Wealth account" means the asset side of your entire balance sheet.

The third 10% and third account is the **Debt account**, and the funds are applied towards your Debt Accelerator. See details below. It should be a checking account.

The 70% and fourth account is your **Bills account** and it contains the money you use for your day-to-day living expenses and for paying bills. It should also be a checking account. In business terminology, it is your operating account.

To summarize, the four Accounts are:

1. 10% Giving—checking account

2. 10% Wealth—savings or brokerage account
3. 10% Debt—checking account
4. 70% Bills/Operating—checking account

Every dollar you receive gets divided into your four accounts based on the 10-10-10-70 Rule. This applies to all earned income as well as any "windfall" money, whether you picked up a dollar off the street, your Aunt Marie sends you $50 for your birthday, you make a big bonus or commissioned sale at work, or you receive a tax refund; *the rule is applied without discretion no matter what.*

Initial deposits go into the seventy percent Bills account. The very first thing you do *before a single bill is paid* is transfer 10% each to your Giving, Wealth, and Debt accounts.

Again, all income, regardless of its source, is allocated according to the ND1 rule: 10% goes to the Giving account, 10% into the Wealth account, 10% to the Debt account, and 70% to the Bills account to cover living expenses. Whenever you receive any amount of money, whether once a week or once a month, the first thing you will do is deposit it into your primary 70% checking account and then do the transfers to your other three dedicated accounts based on the established percentages, while always leaving 70% of the total amount in your primary 70% Bills account.

RESTRUCTURING YOUR BALANCE SHEET FOR CASH FLOW

Now I'm going to let you in on a big secret and central theme of TWF. It's a key strategy of wealthy and elite corporate restructuring specialists but it is not taught in schools or explained by financial planners and advisors. And from my personal experience most of them do not really understand this principle, how powerful it is, and how to properly apply it.

The secret I'm talking about is so powerful because once you understand it, it literally makes you richer and richer *every single year*. And it reduces your stress level. It also makes you what we call resilient or "antifragile" against financial hardship and economic crashes.

What I'm referring to is the process of *restructuring your balance sheet for cash flow*.

This might sound complicated, but once you get it, you'll see how simple it really is and what a crime it is that we aren't taught this in school or by our "advisors."

As a Wealth Builder and practitioner of TWF, we want to learn to optimize our balance sheet for cash flow and that starts with *eliminating all liabilities that aren't directly supporting positive-cash-flow assets*.

HOW TO COMPOUND AND ACCELERATE YOUR DEBT PAYOFF

Referring back to our ND1 formula, 10% of all your earned income goes into your Debt account. This 10% will be your monthly "accelerator" payment (see below) and will fund what we call the **Compound Debt Elimination (CDE) System**. Once all of your debt is eliminated, you will take that 10% and roll it into your Wealth account to further accelerate and compound your cash-flow assets, but first you will use the money to get rid of your debt.

As I keep repeating, *the #1 key to wealth is getting your money working for you instead of you working for your money*. So how does that happen? How do we get our money to work for us? Here's how you do it quickly, efficiently, and consistently.

The first step to getting your money working for you is to eliminate your debt. Debt is a terrible thing because of compound interest working against you. *Consumers are slaves who have compound interest working against them. Wealth Builders are masters who have it working for them.*

As I've pointed out, we live in a global debt-based economy. The terms used to describe economic activity, such as liquidity or credit, all lead back to debt. If you study debt and look into its history, you would have no doubt that it is a form of slavery. If you want freedom, security, and fulfillment in your life, the last thing you want to be is a debt slave. So I'm going to show you how to invert the compound interest that's been working against you your entire life and make it work for you.

We're going to do this through an *accelerator payment*, which will come out of your Debt account (into which you have been putting 10% of your income without fail).

Here's how it works:

COMPOUND DEBT ELIMINATION WORKSHEET

DEBT	BAL	MIN	#PYMTS	PRIORITY	ACC PYMT	NEW # PYMNTS
CC1	2K	$50	40	2	$950	2
CC2	7K	$150	47	4	$1,600	4
Car1	10K	$400	25	1	$900	11
Car2	21K	$500	42	3	$1,450	14
Loan	25K	$300	83	5	$1,900	13
Mort	160K	$1,500	107	6	$3,400/mo	47
Totals	250K		344			91

Example worksheet: Income example $5,000/mo. Accelerator amount = $500/mo.

You start by calculating your monthly gross income. As an example, let's say it's $5,000. 10% of $5,000 is $500, which is the amount of money you will put into your Debt account each month. Your monthly debt accelerator payment is now $500.

Next, you create a spreadsheet or grid of rows and columns that lists all of your debts.

In the first column, you list the types of debt you have, such as car loans, student loans, mortgages, credit cards, medical bills, and so forth.

The second column lists the balance remaining on each debt. In our example, the balances due range between $2,000 and $160,000.

In column three, you list the minimum monthly payment you must make for each debt.

In column four, you list the number of payments you have left in order to pay off the debt by dividing the minimum payment amount into the balance due, which in our illustration ranges from twenty-five to 107 payments. For example, the minimum payment for car #2 is $500. Divide the balance due for car #2, which is $21,000, by $500 and you end up with forty-two payments left to make. The total of all the balances due is $250,000, and the total number of payments left to make is 344.

Next, you assign a priority number for each debt and put it in column five. *Because of the importance of creating momentum, you assign a priority to each debt according to how quickly you can pay off the debt. You make the debt with the fewest remaining payments the top priority*. In the example above, the number one priority is car loan #1, which requires only twenty-five payments in order to pay it off. Next is credit card #1, with forty remaining payments, and so forth.

In column six is the accelerator payment which increases in size when each debt is eliminated.

The last column reflects the new number of payments based on implementing the accelerator system.

In our example CDE, the starting debt accelerator payment is $500. So you take the entire $500 and apply it to the monthly payment for the debt with the number one priority, which in this case is car loan #1. You add the $500 accelerator payment to the monthly car payment of $400 for a total monthly payment of $900. At the same time, *you continue to make the minimum payments on all of your other debts from your 70% bills or operating account*.

Because you are now paying $900 a month for car loan #1, thanks to the addition of the debt accelerator payment, it will now take only eleven payments instead of twenty-five to pay off car loan #1.

Once car loan #1 is paid off, you go to the second priority, which in our example is credit card #1. The minimum monthly payment for credit card #1 is $50. Now we take the $900 that had been used to pay off the car loan and apply it to the credit card #1 payment. So instead of paying $50 a month, we are able to make a monthly payment of $950 on the credit card. That means it will only take two months instead of forty to pay off credit card #1.

Soon, we're on to priority debt number three, which is car loan #2. Instead of paying $500 each month, there is now $1,450 available (the $950 that is freed up from credit card #1 and car loan #1 plus the $400 we would normally use to make the payment). Now things are starting to speed up. Momentum begins to build, which is why we call it an accelerator payment.

The fourth priority is credit card #2, and the amount of the monthly payment has risen to $1,600. So it will only require four payments to pay off credit card #2. And by the time you attack the last priority, the mortgage, the accelerated payment has reached $3,400 a month, and the number of payments needed to pay off the mortgage is reduced to forty-seven from 107.

In our example, *all debts are paid off within seven years, including the mortgage*!

SPEED AND SIMPLICITY RULE

This hypothetical example demonstrates how the CDE or accelerator system works. This example doesn't take into account interest and amortization of the debt, which will affect the exact numbers, but it's simple, and it flat out works because you are compounding the money for debt payoff instead of being the victim of compounded interest on the debt. Clients we've worked with who have applied the CDE system have collectively paid off several millions of dollars of debt.

Some people believe it's more important to pay off high-interest-rate debt first, but that's not necessarily the case. Sometimes it's not only slower but adds complexity. *In all cases, speed and simplicity are the highest priority because they create momentum*!

What makes the TWF Compound Debt Elimination system so powerful and unique is the *psychology* behind it. Remember, personal finance, wealth-building, and investing *without* considering the human nature component are like fighting an 800-pound gorilla. We can think we're smart because we "know" the information, but we're going to lose that fight every time without a superior strategy.

UNSTOPPABLE MOMENTUM

In our example, after only ninety days, momentum starts to build. Once the first debt is paid off, other TWF principles begin to kick into gear. Because you're following the spiritual principles of giving, stewardship, and faithfulness over the small things, paying yourself first, living off of 70%, etc., you start experiencing other breakthroughs and favor in your life, your income starts increasing, and more.

At this point, many people become even more aggressive and apply more money towards debt elimination. Your entire life begins to change. You stop struggling financially, living from paycheck to paycheck and feeling that there's never enough. You are now experiencing serious financial and psychological momentum!

As a Wealth Builder, you'll continue to consistently and methodically apply ND1 on all of your *earned income* after your debts have been paid off so that there's no room for emotions and biases to sabotage your progress towards freedom. The only difference is that once your debt is paid off you're now putting at least 20% monthly into your Wealth account, *which is what the proper ratio should be to begin with.*

WINNING THE BATTLE WHILE LOSING THE WAR

Remember, building wealth is all about *restructuring your balance sheet for cash flow*. Getting out of debt is only the start, the means to the end; *it is not the end itself*. Do not be one of those people who pay off their debt only to rack it right back up again!

I would recommend you read that above paragraph over again and let it sink in. Too many people get excited about paying off their debt, but they don't understand the real war they are in. Missing the bigger picture strategy, they end up back in debt because they didn't understand the real purpose of their money and how to literally make it their slave. *To become free, it's not enough to stop being the slave, you must learn how to become the master.*

POST-DEBT PAYOFF OPTIONS

At this point, if you are fully committed to the TWF process of becoming a Wealth Builder, you have two options:

Minimum option: swear off all new debt and continue living off of 70%, putting 20% now towards your Wealth account.

Aggressive option: swear off all new debt and add the entire total of your newly adjusted "accelerator payment" towards your Wealth account, hyper-compounding and accelerating your asset base, living far below 70% of your earned income.

In strategy 2, the money you set aside for paying off your debts remains off the table. Every month the accelerator payment plus original minimum monthly payments, which in our example had risen to a total of $3,400 per month, gets added to the original 10% wealth amount and now goes into your Wealth account (bringing the total monthly Wealth account allocation far above 20%).

In either case, now the fun really begins! You start compounding your Wealth account and investment growth, and the original goal of getting your money to work for you instead of you working for your money becomes reality. You begin to increase your *unearned income* by rolling the accelerator payment into your Wealth account to fund cash-flow assets, which is the topic we go into in our Assets section.

STOP EATING MENTAL JUNK FOOD

If you're serious about mastering TWF and the debt pillar, you have to accept the fact that you are constantly being influenced by the world around you. All of us are, no one is immune. Even if we think we are smart and independent thinkers, we are still subject to external influences. We have to remain on guard and diligent concerning our social conditioning, proactively take responsibility for it, and learn to use our God-given *free will* to take control of our thoughts, emotions, and lives.

A major influence is television and media in general. From the day we first sat in front of a TV, we began our programming to become a consumer. One day my wife and I decided to put an end to cable television in our family.

We always had a TV in our house, which we used mostly for watching movies as a family.

A number of years ago I was involved in a business startup. Things were going slowly at first. At the end of a long day I'd watch the news and "unwind." I would sit down in front of the screen, thinking I'd watch for thirty minutes or so. Three hours later I would still be there, wondering what happened! *I had been watching, essentially the same thing, repeated over and over by various script-reading talking heads...for three hours*! I'd been completely sucked in and it too easily became a daily habit.

We are not a big sports family, but one year we decided to watch the Super Bowl, which was something we hadn't done for several years. Our kids were young at the time. We were sitting watching the big game when the halftime show came on. It was the one when Janet Jackson did her infamous "wardrobe malfunction" performance. There we were with our four young kids, and that was it! My wife gave me that look (you know the one), then got up and immediately called the cable company and canceled our service. We were done. We never had cable again, and we don't miss it.

About the same time that happened, we started a new business. It was an Internet-based publishing and education company, which went on to become a multimillion-dollar business that dominated its niche. It's still going strong and impacting people's lives today. I'm convinced that the business would never have succeeded like it did if we hadn't canceled our cable TV service. Killing the TV redirected valuable time, brain cells, and energy into that business, which otherwise would have continued going down the mental sewer drain.

If you're still skeptical, you should know that research was done many years ago that suggested watching TV (and likely all forms of passive video media) changes your brain state and lowers your IQ. The ultimate conclusion of the study was open-ended; *they weren't sure if TV made people dumb (causation), or if dumb people just watched a lot of TV (correlation).*

Either way, if you want to be a Wealth Builder, you have

to take proactive action over the kind of media you let eat your time and mind!

Make the decision right now to cut the TV and other addictive media habits. For some this might be consuming large amounts of social media that is sucking up valuable time and energy every day. Habits are difficult if not impossible to break because the mind is always working overtime to move us towards comfort. The easiest way to remove a bad habit is to replace it with a good one. I'd suggest reinvesting that time into learning new skills, which is what I did. You'll never look back and your life will truly never be the same again!

PERCEPTION MARKETING VS BUSINESS MODEL REALITY

The average person consumes seven hours a day of media (TV, radio, Internet, social media, newspapers, magazines, etc.) and is exposed to approximately 10,000 advertising messages daily.

How many of those messages are educating and equipping you to become a Wealth Builder? Unfortunately, the majority are programming you to be a consumer and debt slave, or at best a Rich Miserable Bastard.

I have a background in marketing. Allow me to give you a

sneak peek behind the wizard's curtain and some insight into what's going on.

A marketer's job is to sell, make offers, and offer solutions to problems. If a problem doesn't exist or is unknown, *the marketer will create and agitate desire in the target audience to want or need the solution he has to offer.* A marketer will do whatever it takes to close a sale, whether through traditional media, advertising, social media, or direct response campaigns.

The "news" is no longer about reporting truth or facts anymore. At best, it's become opinion-based entertainment and a vehicle for advertising. That's the business model behind the 24/7 news cycle. In the end, its ultimate purpose is to create content, clicks, and engagement to sell advertising space. Negativity and drama sell. It keeps eyeballs glued (high ratings). Remember this: *the world is an infomercial; everything you see, hear, and read is designed to sell you.* There is no fiduciary responsibility to inform or educate you as the viewer or consumer. It is a business model of content, marketing, and sales; that's it. *The responsibility is to the owners, to maximize shareholder value, not to you the viewer or "consumer."*

This gap or difference between presentation and reality and the need to protect the reputation of an entity versus what's really best for the consumer, widens the larger an organization becomes. This is especially true with large publicly traded corporations run by a board of directors answering to shareholders, to which all major media outlets belong. It is also true of big governments and bureaucracies. There is a *conflict of interest* between profits (or self-preservation) and transparency, and the larger the entity becomes, the bigger that conflict becomes.

Even in smaller unscripted "alternative" media outlets, the business model is ultimately the same. Content must be "created" 24/7. Monetization must happen. Drama, negativity, and fear sell. Truth is subjective at best, presented from the viewpoint of the personality or "influencer." *The market leads the message*; the stronger and more contrarian the opinion, the more passionate and emotional the followers (engagement), the more sales. No sales, no one eats. It's a self-fulfilling feedback loop leading to more and more extremes.

As a Wealth Builder, you must take regular inventory of the media you're consuming. Who and what is influencing you and to what end? Ask yourself honestly, what is the "fruit" of this programming in my life? Again, you'll find 99% is driving you towards stress, anxiety, debt, poverty, consumption, victim identity, and ultimately an unhappy Rich Miserable Bastard life if you do not rein it in!

Production feeds the soul, consumerism starves it. Production not only creates true wealth but is a key factor in quality of life. Too much consumption eats wealth and perverts and distorts happiness and fulfillment. It's natural to want to enjoy the finer things in life and have unforgettable experiences, *but when the cycle of consuming to feel happy takes over, it feeds on itself, creating a black hole that grows bigger and bigger and can never be filled.*

With True Wealth Formula, once you become aware of the influences in your life, apply the Compound Debt Elimination system, and start building your Wealth account, you'll create the foundation to "become the bank" yourself (see Legacy section). You will no longer have to beg for loans or be subject to the whims of interest rates or economic cycles. You will have the means to fund your own business ventures and investments. And you will build a legacy for you and your family.

HOW TO TURN A LIABILITY INTO A CASH-FLOW ASSET

As I've stated several times, we are motivated in life by our emotions. It's human nature to do so. We make emotional and irrational decisions about our money, like when we buy a new car. The excitement we get from buying a car might last ninety days. But the excitement, thrill, fulfillment, and joy you will experience when you add $400 to your Wealth account each and every month will last your entire life. It will never go away. It will build your legacy.

The following story proves my point.

We had an employee once, we'll call him Stephen, who had an old truck that he was tired of and wanted to replace. One day he asked me whether he should buy a new truck. So we sat down and talked about it.

I asked Stephen if his truck was running well and was well maintained.

"Yes," he replied, "it's fine."

"Okay. So what's more important in your life, building wealth or driving a new truck?" I asked, and he replied, "Building wealth."

I explained to him that his vehicle was a liability (technically a depreciating asset) because it cost him money every month to maintain it. I suggested we figure out how to turn his existing truck into a cash-flow asset instead.

We talked about how much the payments would be if he were to buy a new truck, and they would have been between around $400 per month. Then, I suggested he should wear two hats. One hat was going to be the banker's hat, and the other hat would belong to the guy who drives the truck.

Instead of buying a new vehicle, going into debt, and creating negative cash flow, I suggested that he write himself a check each month for $400, which is the amount of money his payments would have been if he had taken out a loan to buy a new truck. After putting that check into his bank account for ninety days, I told him to come back and let me know if he still wanted to buy a new truck. Needless to say, he didn't. The experience changed the trajectory of his life.

Stephen wasn't highly paid at the time, but he learned to adopt the TWF mindset of thinking like the bank. He learned to reposition his liabilities, delay gratification, and take time to think about his goals. He felt empowered, knowing he was on a path to financial independence that could last forever. He now had a system for stepping back and weighing the cost and benefits of new purchases and a method he could apply to future transactions. Instead of making an emotional decision to buy a new truck and get a temporary high that would fade within a few months, he made a strategic decision that was emotionally fulfilling in a completely new and powerful way.

CHAPTER 4

INCOME

THE LAW OF THE SEED

Now I want to give you the oldest and most powerful of all wealth principles. It took me many years to realize the power of this simple truth. If you learn this concept—if you don't let its simplicity fool you but truly catch its depth—it's going to change your relationship with money forever. You'll never look at it the same way again.

Here it is—memorize this law:

> Money is seed. We can either eat it or plant it. When we eat it, it's gone...forever. When we plant it, we can watch it grow into an orchard full of fruit.

Unfortunately, most people eat all the seed, or money, they earn. In this section we'll look at ways to maximize the amount of seed we plant each month while minimizing what we consume. And we'll learn to start producing more than we consume.

If I have a dollar and I *spend* it, I ate it. The seed represented by that dollar is gone; it's dead and went to money heaven. If I plant the seed, or *invest* the dollar, it has the potential to grow into a tree, or into more dollars. If well cared for, it can bear fruit, and the fruit will contain more seeds for planting. In time, all those seeds will grow into a full-blown orchard.

True Wealth Formula is all about understanding the seed. It's about growing an orchard that produces so much fruit that you can walk into the orchard, pick some fruit, eat and enjoy it, and still have plenty of fruit left on the trees. We pay our bills and enjoy the blessings of life, *but we never eat all of our seed*. It's okay to eat some fruit, but not all, because each seed has the potential to become an entire orchard. This is the exact opposite of "modern portfolio theory" retirement planning which we'll talk more about later.

NEVER TOUCH THE PRINCIPAL

The wealthy and those who manage family money through family office structures would refer to a similar concept known as *"never touch the principal."* Meaning, you can use part of the interest to live off of or fund lifestyle but never the principal capital of the estate. This ensures the value of an estate will continue to grow each year for the benefit of successive generations.

The sooner we start planting money seeds, the sooner we'll have an orchard that lasts for generations. We'll experience more happiness and fulfillment while gaining financial independence, and we'll have learned how to be happier with less.

To be clear, time and patience are invaluable resources. Compounding isn't very exciting for the first 10 years, then it starts to get interesting and momentum builds. By year 20, in almost every compound interest chart you look at, things start to go vertical. The classic "hockey stick" pattern of charts and graphs starts to show up and our orchard is in full force!

INCOME VS. WEALTH

Now let's discuss how to optimize our *earned* income, or the money we work for. If you do what we advise in this section, you will double your income at a minimum. In some cases, depending on the person, industry, and business model, ten times or more income is possible. That may sound unrealistic, but we've seen it happen with our clients many times.

There are two types of income: earned income and unearned income.

The wealthy minimize their earned income and maximize their unearned income. The middle class and poor do the opposite. They spend their entire lives working for money instead of getting their money to work for them.

We've repeatedly made the statement: the #1 key to wealth is to get your money working for you instead of you working for your money. This is a central concept of the TWF system. The money we work for is our *earned income*. The money that works for us is our *unearned income*. TWF shifts the focus and momentum towards the unearned-income portion of your Wealth account, freeing you to "work" for contribution, fulfillment, joy, and legacy instead of for money.

Having an income, however, does not necessarily mean the same thing as having wealth. People who drive fancy cars and live in big houses are often not the wealthiest, no matter what the media presents to the contrary. As the best-selling book *The Millionaire Next Door* put it, *people who look rich usually aren't*.

You'll often hear people talk about how well they're doing, throwing around six- or seven-figure numbers. They'll use gross income figures but not net. They don't talk about, or even know, how their assets and liabilities show up on their balance sheet nor do they discuss liquid net worth or "return on assets." This is a key distinction between those who are easily impressed with high income figures and those who know and understand what real wealth is.

Like with debt, when dealing with income, we start with our mindset. First, we get our thinking straightened out so that our behaviors and habits change.

True wealth is not about flashy displays of money and lifestyle. *TWF defines wealth as financial independence, which means your assets are generating more income than you do personally.* When you reach this goal, you've essentially achieved financial freedom and can now invest your time into your passions, life goals, and the relationships that matter most to you.

YOUR MOST IMPORTANT ASSET

Your Balance Sheet shows whether your net worth is positive or negative, and whether your assets are greater or less than your liabilities. *In simple non-accounting terms, your Balance Sheet is everything you own minus everything you owe.* If the value of what you own is greater than what you owe, you have a positive net worth. If it's less, then you have a negative net worth. In a business, net worth is called equity.

When we work with our clients, I'll ask them to make a list of all the income-producing assets they have, such as stocks, bonds, a rental property, a part-time business, and so forth. The one thing no one ever puts on their list is their own name, and that's the very thing that should be first on the list!

This goes to the heart of a major problem with accounting. There is no recognition of the fact that every person starts out life with a balance sheet of zero.

We all begin life in exactly the same position. The only thing on our balance sheet is our name—who we are as a person, our mind, our thinking patterns, how we see the world, our ability to solve problems, our ability to produce value in the marketplace, and our ability to connect with people and make contacts.

We all also end the same way. We're all going to die one day, and none of us will be able to take anything with us when we do.

People have different skills, abilities, talents, and the possibility to change. We can all improve ourselves, learn new skills, increase our knowledge, and choose whom we'll associate with (the power of association is a big factor in how we think and see the world).

Accounting fails to take into account any of those important facts. No one sits down with a CPA and has a conversation about how to increase the most valuable asset on his or her balance sheet, which is ourselves. The accountant never puts the client's name on the balance sheet (most accountants and financial advisors have very little understanding or experience with intellectual property or intangible assets).

THREE TYPES OF ECONOMIES

Earned income comes from the work you do to make money. Unearned income comes from money that works for you. Generally speaking, unearned income is taxed less than earned income.

There are three types of economies: the time-for-money economy (TFM), the results-for-money economy (RFM), and the money-for-money economy (MFM).

We are all familiar with the TFM economy. That's the one in which we trade our time for money. It's typically earned as wages or salary and generally reported via W2 or 1099 in the case of a US citizen's tax return. This is generally linear income. If I make $10 an hour and I work 10 hours, I have $100. If I make $1,000 an hour and don't go to work, I make zero dollars. In the TFM economy, even if I increase my skills and value to the marketplace and increase my income, it's still a linear income limited to the time I show up to work.

The main problem with the TFM economy is that every one of us is limited by the number of hours there are in a day. There is only so much time we can spend working. Still, if you're in this economy there is always a lot of room for income growth by increasing your skillset and value to the market. There are many high-income earners in the TFM economy.

In the RFM economy, you get paid according to the results you create, not for your time (you can show up and work all day, but if you don't make a sale for example, you make no money). Income is often earned as tips, commissions, or bonuses and often but not always reported via W2, 1099, or Schedule C. The RFM economy also includes the potential for leverage. If you learn to create a bigger and more valuable result, you'll increase your income. There are many other RFM economy examples besides sales, like some creative roles, product development, marketing and advertising, management, networking and putting deals together, active stock trading, real estate flips, and most small businesses or startups, just to name a few.

EARNED INCOME CREATES THE SEED MONEY

An important point: *the earned-income skill, whether in the time-for-money or results-for-money economies, creates the initial seed money for the unearned income.* Typically, you want to quickly develop skills in the RFM economy (move as quick as possible from TFM to RFM) because RFM often (not always) is a faster path to developing unearned income, which is the road to financial independence and the goal of TWF.

Both the TFM and RFM economies are *earned* income. The MFM economy is *unearned* income. It's where our assets are creating cash-flow income and capital growth for us. Income reported on Schedule B, D, or E of our 1040 return (if you're a US citizen) is typically "unearned income," but not always.

Note: I am not using the term "unearned income" or giving reporting examples as official accounting terms or tax reporting advice. They are simply being provided as examples to keep things simple and consistent with our core TWF definitions and also to give you some familiarity of the different types of income and how they might be reported and flow into a tax return. Again this may be different in your specific country or situation, but the general concept of earned and unearned income applies even though different terms may be used (e.g., passive income, portfolio income, etc.)

HOW TO NOT GET FIRED

If you want more income, you have to find ways to increase your capacities in order to earn more. You do this through increasing your value to the marketplace.

Remember this law: *the marketplace pays for value.*

To illustrate, let's look at entitlement mentality. Many people feel they should be paid a certain wage for doing their jobs. They want a minimum wage or some form of guaranteed income.

The flaw with this thinking is that it fails to take into account the employer's perspective. The reason an employer hires an employee is to solve a problem or fill a need, period. No business hires employees simply because they want an employee. On the balance sheet of large corporations, employees are viewed as liabilities. An employee should be considered an asset if cultivated and treated like one, but lots of companies don't see it that way.

A prime example is when there's an economic downturn or a company has financial problems. One of the first things a company does under those circumstances is to lay people off. Payroll offers one of the easiest ways to cut costs. A company lets people go so that it can reduce expenses and increase cash flows and profit margins.

When publicly traded companies do this their stock often rises because again, they're reducing "liabilities" on the balance sheet. So I would encourage you to take yourself as your most valuable asset very seriously and invest accordingly. At a minimum, if you're an employee, it will serve as an insurance policy and help keep you in the "asset" column of your company.

HOW TO INCREASE YOUR EARNED INCOME

The marketplace pays for value. There are four ways to increase your value in the marketplace so your income goes up:

1. Knowledge
2. Skill
3. Contacts
4. Action

If a person has specialized **Knowledge** in a particular area and is able to use that knowledge in a productive way to solve problems in the marketplace, he'll be more highly valued and receive more income. However, knowledge alone is not enough without at least one of the others. By itself, it is the weakest of the four to rely on.

The second is **Skill**. Having and developing a skillset in sales, for example, can lead to doubling, tripling, or even

10x-ing income. After getting an education, many people fail to consider what more they could learn. They don't think about new problems they could solve or new habits they could master. They don't continue to develop, learn, and grow.

This often leads to entitlement thinking, which is based on the belief that we're owed something. I'm owed a pay raise or a promotion after 20 years of work. Congress should pass a new minimum wage law for my benefit, etc. It leads to a victim identity and expecting others to solve our problems. True Wealth Formula shuns victim identity in favor of taking personal responsibility and asking the right questions. *Remember, no one will do for you what you are not willing to do for yourself!*

We must actively apply ourselves to learn new skills as we transition fully out of the industrial age and into an age of increasing technology, innovation, disruption, and "creative destruction."

There's no time to wait for someone else to solve your income problems or for thinking you're owed a handout or a hand-up. There's no time for expecting old jobs to come back. The world will keep moving forward; *you should be thinking about who you want to be in five years' time.* What you know now is already outdated, and your skills are becoming obsolete with every passing day.

This is where being mindful of the larger big-picture trends is helpful. You are not going to stop these trends. *The new economy requires a mindset of adaptability and flexibility. You have to become mentally tough and resilient. With great change comes great opportunity and the most valuable skillset will always be the ability to identify and solve problems.*

A third way to increase income is through **Contacts**. Not everyone has specialized knowledge or a particular skillset, but they could become an incredible networker. Some of us have a gift for meeting people, networking, making contacts, brokering deals, or making introductions. That's the type of person who's always in the middle of things. The value such a person brings to the marketplace comes from relationships and the ability to meet new people and connect people to others.

The fourth way to increase income is through **Action**. A person just starting out in life often lacks specialized knowledge, a well-developed skillset, or contacts. In such a case, that person should focus on excelling and increasing their income through taking "all-out massive action," providing amazing service and work ethic.

By taking action, I mean the person is not lazy. He shows up for work early instead of on time or late like many people do. He goes the extra mile, gives 110%, smiles, does his work with a spirit of excellence, and focuses his attention on solving problems. Promotions, better advancement opportunities, recruitment by other departments or companies will present themselves to him and bring with them the possibility for acquiring specialized knowledge, learning new skills, and making contacts. As an employer, I'm going to pick the guy or gal with a strong work ethic and a heart to go the extra mile over the person who thinks they know everything but can't get anything done. One key to massive action is your mindset as well as your physical energy level. Taking care of yourself, good diet, and exercise are important.

Unfortunately, many young people coming out of school with a degree think they're entitled to a salary simply for what they know. They often lack a work ethic that may be of more benefit in the marketplace than what they learned in school.

People excel in different areas. If you want to earn more money, you're going to have to learn to solve bigger problems through knowledge, skill, contacts, or action.

Remember this law: *the bigger the problem, the bigger the paycheck.*

If you're not happy with the size of your paycheck, start focusing on solving bigger problems.

LEARNING HOW TO LEARN

Conventional wisdom says you go to school, get an education, and find a good job.

The problem with this mindset is that it assumes the educational process has a start date and an end date; that once it's done, it's done for good. Unfortunately, this thinking leads people to believe that once they've joined the workforce, there's no need to learn anything more.

The Wealth Builder believes that the most valuable form of education is self-education, which may or may not include the conventional route of going to college and getting a degree. Even more importantly, it emphasizes *falling in love with learning* and taking responsibility for our ongoing educational process.

Learning how to learn will become one of the most valuable assets you can acquire. Again, the new economy is moving and evolving quickly, and it requires a mindset of adaptability and flexibility. So we have to ask ourselves: if I want to increase my income over the next ten years, what do I need to learn now, starting today, in order to do that? What new knowledge will help me solve bigger problems?

Today, it's a lot easier to self-educate than it's ever been before, thanks to technology. Now you don't have to spend four to five years going six figures into debt to pay school loans in order to acquire specialized knowledge and skills. You can go online and find many of the courses you could ever want at a fraction of the cost.

DO THIS INSTEAD OF JUST PAYING BILLS

Another way to self-educate and advance your earning power is by looking for opportunities to work for people who have the skillsets you want and learn from them. The mentor/apprentice model has been the bedrock of developing technical skill and craftsmanship for centuries, but the concept can also be applied to many other areas of skill development.

When looking for work, *the Wealth Builder prioritizes jobs that provide opportunities for making contacts or gaining specialized knowledge and skill rather than just the highest salary.* That way your job becomes an investment in yourself, which as you now know, will always be the most important asset on your balance sheet. If you only work to pay the bills, that's all you'll ever do. Even if you aren't making the biggest salary, you could pick the brain of a self-made millionaire for five or six years. Experience like that will end up paying significantly more dividends over time than a temporarily better-paying position that doesn't teach you anything new.

There's also the possibility that even if you make great

money, you'll end up just becoming the Rich Miserable Bastard who lacks true fulfillment and personal growth, which are fundamental to having a meaningful life. Always remember that *you are your number one asset*, and that investing in education is invaluable. Like owning a stock, you should *ask yourself every day, is my value is going up or down*. When you invest in your biggest asset, yourself, it will pay dividends forever.

HOW NOT TO BE REPLACED BY A MACHINE

Another reason to fall in love with learning early and to get in the habit of self-educating is to increase your ability to adapt to today's incredibly fast-changing world. Within a matter of years, whole industries and professions will become obsolete. Technology is changing every sector of the economy—energy, finance, construction, transportation, communication, politics, entertainment, and more. The rate of innovation and disruption is accelerating exponentially. Being adaptable is a core TWF mindset and essential to thriving when things change rapidly. Adaptability is becoming a preeminent quality in the new economy.

Five years ago, for example, I had eleven designers, developers, and programmers working in our company to manage software code and develop websites. Several were independent contractors and about half were employees, which created substantial overhead costs and liability on the company balance sheet. Today it just takes a few clicks to access software on the Internet that does the same thing as those eleven people. One would have thought that the skills of a web designer or a programmer would be secure in the new economy, but they weren't *unless* they adapted and evolved, as the marketplace is constantly shifting with newer, better technologies emerging.

Self-driving vehicles are another example. The transportation industry will be changing radically in the next few years. Human beings will no longer be needed in many truck-driving roles. The transportation of goods will become completely automated, which hopefully will mean fewer accidents and deaths on the road. If I were a truck driver today and it was my only skill, I'd be spending every hour that I was driving the truck listening to audio courses so I could reprogram my mind and learn new skills. I'd be reading books at every truck stop that dealt with skills for the future to help me tackle a new and bigger problem than driving a truck, and I'd be attending every seminar and conference I could to invest in myself and increase my knowledge, skill, contacts, and action-oriented mindset. And I'd have a side hustle to stress-test those new skills and perfect my craft.

Here's a key point; when you fall in love with learning,

embrace the challenge of adapting to change and abandoning the idea of just working to pay bills, "work" is no longer work but an opportunity for growth *which is fulfilling in and of itself.* You've just changed the entire trajectory of your life and you are already experiencing part of the Wealth Builder lifestyle.

Again, in order to survive this era of rapid change, you'll need a high degree of adaptability, which means your education will never be over. Better to fall in love with learning and personal development now and enjoy the journey. Once you do, you'll never look back!

ABSORB WHAT IS USEFUL

Bruce Lee, the famous martial artist and film star, has long been an inspiration of mine. His art and philosophy of Jeet Kune Do (JKD) is deeply embedded within TWF. A key tenet of JKD—"absorb what is useful, reject what is useless, add what is specifically your own"—should be adopted by the serious Wealth Builder. Lee promoted continuous self-improvement. He said you need to be like water so that you can adapt to your environment.

Lee was a visionary and innovator who promoted a radical thought at the time...*the idea that the individual is more important than the system.* In today's MMA (mixed martial arts) environment, this isn't too radical an idea anymore.

It's common knowledge that when you're talking about combat, especially if it's on the street or in war, you absolutely MUST adapt strategy and tactics that work and get results. You cannot hold on to tradition for the sake of honor while you're getting your ass kicked or worse. You must be adaptable, and you must be forward-thinking with an offensive mindset. In the end, it's you against your opponent or environment. Resilience, forward pressure, and flexibility are essential qualities of the Wealth Builder.

Life sucks sometimes. It doesn't usually go the way we want. It's absolutely critical to adapt and learn from every experience and every mistake. When a mistake happens, step back and think: What can I learn from this? How can I make sure I don't repeat this mistake again? *How do I make that mistake my slave and pay me dividends for the rest of my life*? When you ask good questions like those, you'll find all the answers you'll need.

There are endless opportunities to self-educate. Fall in love with learning and make the decision right now to become a lifelong learner!

NEW ECONOMY POWER SKILLS

Power skills are skills that offer leverage. Unlike linear skillsets that have a one-to-one ratio, power skills are geometric, which means they have a multiplier effect. There is no limit to how much they can potentially increase your income.

There are a number of power skills that can equip you for success in the new economy. At the center are critical thinking skills, creative problem-solving, and people skills. Here are a few examples.

SALES

Some people cringe when they think of sales, but it's the oldest profession in the world. Every human being, whether they realize it or not, is involved in sales in one way or another. Most people, however, aren't good at sales because they have misconceived perceptions about it.

No matter who you are or where you live, you are involved in at least one of the four areas of sales. You are either:

- Selling a product
- Selling a service
- Selling an idea
- Or you're selling yourself

Someone who's an administrator may think he has nothing to do with sales. But every day that he shows up for work, he's selling himself: his performance; his attitude; whether he smiles or frowns; whether he's involved in gossip, politicking, or backbiting; whether he's diligent and a team player; or whether he creates more value for the company. *How you perform, your heart, your smile, and your spirit of excellence are all part of selling yourself.* If you don't sell yourself daily in a positive way, you'll end up on the short list when the company goes through tough times and looks for employees to lay off.

If you're a stay-at-home mom, you're in sales, too. You're selling your kids on eating their vegetables every night for dinner, and that requires a top-notch sales pitch. If your kids whine and cry about eating their veggies, then you're probably not good at sales. You'll want to learn the skill of persuasion so you can instill an eager desire in your kids to eat vegetables.

Sales is a skill that everyone can benefit from. Every professional will improve by learning to sell better. Business owners, and entrepreneurs especially, need to master all aspects of selling, including how to prospect, present, close, follow up, and follow through, as well as provide solid customer service and cultivate referrals.

If you're lacking in sales skills, you should be immediately looking for opportunities to develop this area, but as a professional, not an amateur. If you do, you will without doubt see your income increase, regardless of your current job or profession: it's guaranteed. Dani Johnson, my amazing wife and business partner of 25 years, has helped tens of thousands increase their income. She is literally the best I know at helping people increase their income through mastery of this skill *as well as many other income-boosting and life skillsets.*

MARKETING

Marketing, which is related to sales, is a high-leverage set of skills that includes advertising, lead generation, direct marketing, copywriting, branding, and positioning. Knowing how to write a compelling advertisement or a headline, craft an irresistible offer, identify and test different price points, put together a presentation, articulate benefits, and upsell, down-sell, and cross-sell, whether in writing, verbally, or with video, are all part of the marketing skillset.

You can learn marketing power skills in many ways: through books, audios, home study courses, mentoring, seminars and courses, coaching programs, and working alongside veteran marketing professionals who've mastered the skillset. In my book and course *eMarketing Formula*, I cover the Internet Business and Marketing skillset in detail.

PEOPLE AND COMMUNICATION SKILLS

Whether you're a project manager, a customer service

representative, or a professional executive, you interact with people to some degree. The higher up the management ladder in a company you are, the greater the value placed on excellent conflict resolution and communication skills will be. High-level corporate executives are primarily engaged in communication.

Everyone benefits from mastering the fundamentals of communication. With up to 93% of communication being nonverbal, there's much to be learned about how we communicate and the messages we send.

If you have poor communication and people skills, your income will not rise above a certain level. This is because no man is an island. We need others to help us get where we're going. If our people skills suck, we're going to cap our growth considerably.

PROJECT MANAGEMENT

Project management is another valuable power skill in the new economy because of the large proportion of work being done via off-site remote teams. A person with excellent project management skills brings more value to the marketplace. Being able to manage people, budgets, timelines, schedules, tasks, and projects entails a combination of communication and sales skills, as well as good organization skills and technical know-how.

The ability to efficiently manage complex projects with lots of moving parts and pieces, without dropping the ball, is high value to every business.

PUBLIC SPEAKING

Public speaking is necessary in coaching, team-building, motivating people, training employees, making presentations, and assuming leadership. Especially in sales, if you've conquered the fear of speaking publicly, you'll succeed well in all aspects of your job.

Pursuing a career as a public speaker also offers high income potential. You become a good public speaker by taking advantage of every opportunity to make presentations, do trainings, and address groups large and small. It can be helpful to keep a journal of your speaking experiences and to learn from and model those who are skilled presenters and public speakers.

ACCOUNTING

The power skills associated with accounting include tax planning, legal structuring, number crunching, financial management, and investing. Whether you're an individual investor, an entrepreneur, or an employee of a company, accounting skills will prove valuable.

Many people are intimidated by numbers and don't understand accounting or the tax code. By becoming knowledgeable in accounting, finance, and legal structuring, you'll be better equipped to spot problems and opportunities, avoid mistakes and liabilities, and save money. Your value to a company or yourself will increase substantially by expanding in this area even just a little bit.

GROW AND SCALE A BUSINESS

Being able to grow and scale a business is a power skill. Similar in ways to project management, this skillset is more closely related to process optimization. You'll increase efficiency and productivity at least two or three times by being able to identify and remove bottlenecks. Whether by eliminating a choke point, streamlining a process, or assessing employees' strengths and weaknesses, you'll be able to help a business double in size through improving its efficiency.

BE EMPLOYEE-PRENEURIAL

Employee-preneurial reflects the mindset of an employee who has the attitude of an entrepreneur without feeling entitled. An employee-preneur realizes that business owners hire employees because they have problems to be solved. An employee-preneur is not one who works minimum hours to avoid being fired or looks out only for himself as he climbs his way to the top.

An employee-preneur has a mindset like the owner of the business. He takes responsibility for everything that goes on in the company. He doesn't complain or gossip and strives to improve his skills and enlarge his contacts. He shows up for work looking to give, not take; he focuses on solving problems not creating them; he is a producer, not a consumer.

Having the mindset of an employee-preneur will change your performance. Opportunities and doors will begin to open up, and you'll become a valuable person to the company. If a position becomes available, the employee-preneur will be offered the promotion or the opportunity to start a new division of the company. He has *freed his mind* from the labels of his job description, and his income will grow as a consequence. He has adopted the mindset of the results for money (RFM) economy, and it will pay dividends and provide leverage.

THE RETIREMENT MYTH

True Wealth Formula doesn't embrace the conventional modern perspective on retirement. Retirement is fundamentally an idea that originated from the industrial age. Developed in the early 1900s, it was a response to working in a factory for 40 hours a week for 40 years of your life. When workers became too old to work, they were given a gold watch and a Winnebago, and hopefully they had enough good health left to drive around and see the grandkids before dying.

The entire financial planning industry is based on that type of thinking. Unfortunately, for many it hasn't worked so well. Most financial decisions are geared towards retirement; portfolio allocations are based on age, income level, expenses, and risk tolerance instead of defining and designing a fulfilling life.

People are often miserable after they retire, and life expectancy diminishes rapidly. Others just don't want to retire, and if they do, they become unhappy. People spend life preparing for "retirement," then once they're there, it's not what it's cracked up to be. They often go back to work to make ends meet financially or out of boredom and loneliness.

Why spend your entire life chasing a concept that statistically isn't working for most people? Follow the old ways that have worked for thousands of years, adopt the TWF mindset and lifestyle, reach financial independence early in life then invest your latter years following your passion and helping others. Your retirement years should be the most productive and wise years of your life. The last thing you should do is sit at home and watch TV all day. You have far too much value to offer this world!

By following the True Wealth Formula, you'll have financial independence and be a healthy, productive person with a gratifying life long before retirement age. And you'll be able to give back to your family and community during what should be your golden years because you've developed unearned income to meet your needs and you're now free to mentor others and help them grow. If you're already in retirement age, you can use the principles in TWF to create a legacy that outlives you, starting with sharing this book and its ideas with others.

FUN, ADVENTURE, AND LIFESTYLE

Where will you be in five years' time? If you don't dedicate yourself to learning new skills and changing your mindset, odds are you'll probably be exactly where you are today. By adopting the TWF mindset and becoming a lifelong learner, you'll live a life full of adventure, growth, and fulfillment.

If you learn a six-digit skillset, the money will come. If that's your goal, it's guaranteed to happen. In business, it's sometimes easier to go from a six-figure income to a seven-figure income than it is to get to six figures in the first place (depending on the business model). The progression doesn't generally proceed in even increments; a jump occurs. When you're on the path of self-education, solving bigger problems, learning specialized skills, developing contacts, and cultivating a strong work ethic, you'll begin to experience exponential leaps in your life. And you'll enjoy a fun and adventurous lifestyle at the same time!

COMPOUND SKILL DEVELOPMENT WORKSHEET

As a Wealth Builder, you start to become intimately familiar with your balance sheet and the relationship between your assets and liabilities. The three pillars of Debt, Income, and Assets structure your life.

The following TWF Compound Skill Development (CSD) worksheet will help you develop and compound your skills. You can create leverage and income-generating momentum in the same way that the CDE worksheet inverts compound interest to accelerate getting rid of debt.

COMPOUND SKILL DEVELOPMENT WORKSHEET

INCOME DESC	MO AMT	A/P	L/G	SKILLS	TIME	UPSIDE	SECURE	PORTABLE

First, list all of your income-producing assets. Number one on the list, of course, will be your name. Next list all of your core skills. Then list any other income-producing assets you may have, such as a rental property or stocks and bonds. Next you rate your assets according to their value, or income generated monthly. You consider whether it's active income, such as a salary, or passive income, like rent received from owning an apartment building. Some of your skills will have more value than others. A portable income skill, such as freelance writing, could be of higher value than a non-portable one because it offers you greater geographical freedom and scalability than a well-paid job that keeps you pinned down to an office building in a particular city for the rest of your life.

You also want to consider whether a skill has leverage,

whether it's a linear skill or a geometric skill. If it's a geometric skill, such as sales, marketing, or project management, it has the potential to double, triple, or quadruple your income.

Once you have completed the worksheet, you identify which skills have the most capacity for leverage and will get you where you want to be in five years' time. As you focus on them, you'll compound your skills and create geometric growth in your income.

THE CROSSFIRE PRINCIPLE

The TWF crossfire principle is a method for driving down debt at the same time you increase income. It's a form of creating a pressure squeeze that has origins in military tactics.

In combat, you never want to get into a situation where your enemy is flanking you and you are pinned down in crossfire. That's the death zone. Unfortunately, that's where many people live their financial lives. They're caught in the crossfire of debt and paying compound interest. *True Wealth Formula flips the tables on this scenario by creating a situation that identifies debt as the enemy, pins it down with the CDE, and strangles it with the additional forward pressure of rising income.*

While you're driving down your debt (with the CDE worksheet), at the same time you'll increase your income by developing your power skills and creating more value in the marketplace, which will create a wedge or crossfire that hits the problem from two angles. Because of our ND1 10/10/10/70 formula, you'll accelerate debt payoff and asset accumulation simultaneously. This will result in shortening the amount of time it will take to go from working for your money to having your money work for you, and it can happen very quickly when applying the concepts outlined in this book.

The essential idea of the crossfire principle is to create a snowball effect for converting debt into wealth through simultaneously increasing income and decreasing debt, which in turn creates momentum for developing your wealth-building machine. The gap between your cost of living and your debt will go directly into your assets, with your assets beginning to spin off more and more cash flow (which we'll discuss in the next chapter), compounding your wealth even further.

Increasing income speeds up the entire process and puts everything into hyperdrive, because it's all about ratios and *following the formulas given in this book.* When you increase your income, the amounts applied towards your Wealth account and debt-accelerator payments grow also!

TAX EFFICIENCY

Taxes will always be the biggest expense in your life. Most people think paying taxes is a necessary evil and don't give enough thought to tax planning or to optimizing their tax situation. The Wealth Builder knows he needs to work towards tax efficiency.

Having 40% of your income (actually a lot more when all city, state, and federal taxes are added up) go to paying taxes every year is a big incentive for learning how to lessen the tax bite in every legal way possible. Be willing to learn everything you can about taxes and pay good experts to help you.

Tax-efficiency techniques include the implementation of structures such as corporations, LLCs, and trusts; knowing how to document things properly so that deductions can be taken; being familiar with how the tax code is written; and understanding that the tax code favors business owners and penalizes employees.

Employee-preneurs may want to consider starting a part-time business. Not only does a part-time business provide an opportunity for increasing your earned income, it can also offer deductions otherwise unavailable to a W2 employee. Even more opportunity may be available with a C corporation, an LLC, or other legal entities that provide asset protection and help with overall tax planning.

Working with experts is important. An accountant knows the various deductions that can be taken, but those that specialize in legal strategic tax planning can be invaluable. Every dollar that you can deduct is a dollar in your pocket. Don't be afraid to pay for good advice in addition to educating yourself about taxes. If you know how to ask the right questions, you'll be able to discern when you're receiving good or bad information.

Some say it's our patriotic duty to pay a lot of taxes. I would argue that minimizing our tax liabilities helps us reinvest directly back into the economy (where we have more direct control over our business or investment activities) and is actually much more patriotic than giving money to an unaccountable bureaucracy. We should always pay 100% of whatever tax we legally owe. Be sure to report and disclose things properly and be careful of tax scheme promoters and unnecessary complexity. If you don't understand it, don't do it. Remember you have ultimate responsibility, not your attorney or CPA. Regardless of what they recommend, you are liable.

EXTREME OWNERSHIP

Things were hard when we first started out in business. I didn't have confidence dealing with numbers. I was under the impression that in order to be a good entrepreneur and business owner we had to outsource and delegate.

I was operating under the common assumption that we should focus solely on what we're good at and let others do everything else.

My background and key areas of expertise were in marketing, product development, branding, and positioning. That's what I was good at. For many years we hired experts and expected them to take care of the accounting, bookkeeping, and even managing our investments. After a while, we began to realize a lot of mistakes were being made. There was little attention to detail and in the end, we were paying for mistakes and incurring the liability of someone else's errors. We realized too much trust was being put into the recommendation of experts and things were too complex to be kept in good order.

Eventually, I came to accept the fact that no one was going to care about our business or management of our money more than I would. Sound familiar?

I bit the bullet and started reading everything I could get my hands on about accounting and tax planning. I met with all kinds of tax nerds and forced myself to ask questions so that I could learn. Over time, things started to click.

Today I'm a firm believer that anyone who sincerely wants to understand accounting and tax efficiency can.

If you care enough, you'll invest the time it takes to learn, and the sooner you do, the better!

BECOME AN ENTREPRENEUR

Historically, private business is the number one creator of wealth. Real estate is usually number two, followed by stocks (ownership in publicly traded companies) and bonds (loans made to publicly traded companies, municipalities, and governments).

If you want the potential to exponentially grow income, consider starting a business and becoming an entrepreneur. It's high-risk (most businesses fail), but it's easier to start a business today than ever before. Startup costs are much less than they used to be, and the potential is huge. Years ago, a startup would take millions to get off the ground. Now the number is $5,000 or less. This is why you're seeing so many recent startups hitting one-billion-dollar valuations (think Uber, Airbnb, Slack, etc.), because they're able to get off the ground and prove concept, then grow via private equity, crowdsourcing, or angel and venture capital investors. Fewer companies are going public to raise capital and grow; times are changing. Markets are no longer constrained by geography, and it's no longer necessary to open a brick-and-mortar store or sign a year's lease. Access to information, training, knowledge, and education is extensive.

The key is to start asking the right questions, figure out which problems need solving, and look for opportunities in niches you are familiar with. This is how we launched our first big product that took our business to seven figures. It was a simple book of sales scripts in a hungry market, an unscratched itch and big problem that no one else with proven expertise was addressing ("what do I say when..."). Our clients' results went through the roof, some who'd never had success before. Later this opened doors to other hungry markets and more growth.

Many successful businesses begin from the simple desire to earn money. You might begin by becoming an affiliate or a sales representative for a home business, which can help cross the bridge from being an employee to becoming an entrepreneur. Be willing to try and not afraid to fail.

FAIL YOUR WAY TO SUCCESS

Fear of failure stops many people. The key to success in the new economy is to go from idea to market quickly. Your goal should not be success but *if you're going to fail, fail fast*. Test ideas quickly. The market is feedback; each time you try, you're learning a new skill and getting experience that's going to be leveraged for the rest of your life, maybe not in the same business or venture, but in another one you can't see right now. So it's back to mindset; you have to be resilient and willing to experiment and try. Fail quick = success. That's not logical, but it's the truth. And it's the mindset of the Wealth Builder and TWF practitioner.

Starting a business provides a great opportunity for learning new skills of all kinds—sales, marketing, people skills, presentation skills, leadership skills, project management. Don't work a job just to pay your bills; *if you're going to work a job, any job, work to learn new skills.*

If your business succeeds and becomes successful, it will benefit your family for generations to come. Your kids and grandkids could work part-time after school and start learning valuable skills. There are many advantages in developing and growing a family business. You'll be on your way to creating a legacy that could last for generations.

Look around you. Even in your current job or career, there are probably hidden opportunities for growth everywhere. Don't rely on others to notice you or give you a handout or opportunity. That's the mindset of the victim. Just put your head down, go to work, and focus on solving problems and creating value. Smile. Encourage others. Start investing in yourself by attending conferences and training seminars. Read books like this one. Trust me, people will notice.

CHAPTER 5

ASSETS

RESTRUCTURING THE BALANCE SHEET FOR CASH FLOW

Once debt is eliminated, your income is rising, and you're consistently applying the TWF ND1 formula for earned income, you're going to see your Wealth account start growing fast. This is where you begin to work on cash-flow assets. This is the point at which you start making the transition from working for money (earned income) to your money working for you (unearned income). Having put the systems and controls in place for reducing spending and increasing income, you'll now have money available for building and developing a strong asset base and creating a powerhouse balance sheet.

Building a solid base of assets begins with restructuring your balance sheet. You'll want to minimize or eliminate your liabilities or debt. *If you do have any liabilities, they should be backed by cash-flow assets.*

As we said at the beginning of the Income Pillar section, money is seed. We either eat our seed or we plant it. Our goal is to plant as much seed as we can and reduce the amount we eat or consume. Once we eat our seed, it's gone—forever. When we plant our seed, there's the potential for the seed to grow into a massive fruit-producing orchard.

By restructuring your balance sheet the right way, you'll create a situation where over time you'll have an entire orchard of assets that will continue to produce cash flow year after year after year.

ASSETS VS LIABILITIES

It's been said that an asset puts money in your pocket, while a liability takes money out of your pocket. That sounds good, but let's get a bit more specific.

If we refer back to the Money Quadrant chart in the Debt Pillar, it lays out the four quadrants of assets and liabilities. Let's review them again because this is central to the wealth-building process.

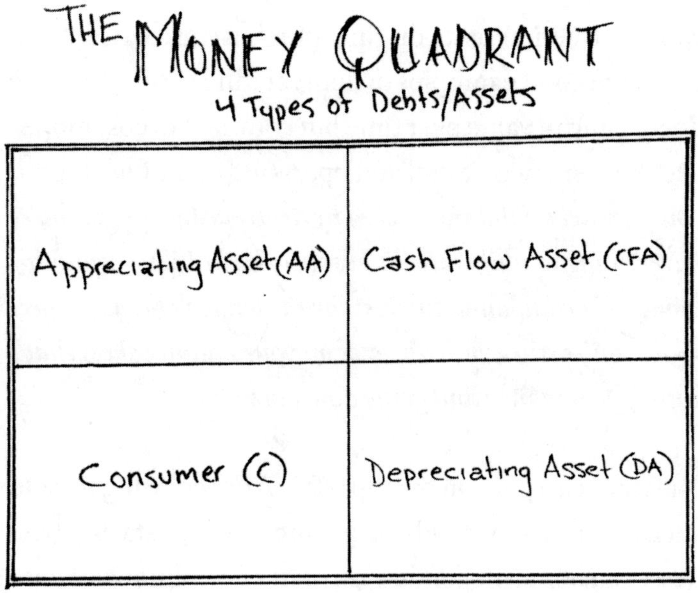

On the bottom left of the chart is **Consumer Debt**, which produces no assets and only liabilities (like credit card debt) on your balance sheet. Your money is completely consumed by the purchases you made. You have nothing left to show for it on your balance sheet. You've either used up or thrown away whatever it was that you purchased, leaving you only with the debt liability to pay off.

On the bottom right are **Depreciating Assets**. An example of a depreciating asset is rent-to-own furniture, which produces a negative cash flow via a rental agreement, which is considered a legally binding liability on your balance sheet. When the terms of the lease are settled or paid in full, you're left with old used furniture that's now worth a fraction of its original purchase price. Cars and boats are good examples of depreciating assets; they are decreasing in value over time but continue to cost money via maintenance, taxes, and operating or storage fees. *If you have debt liabilities backed by depreciating assets, you're never going to build wealth because the liability is making money via compound interest for the lender's balance sheet while you're stuck with an asset on your balance sheet that's costing you money and going down in value.*

The third category on the top left is **Appreciating Assets**, such as land, non-dividend-paying stocks, a startup business, or a home (depending on market conditions). These types of assets are akin to gambling. There's no guarantee you'll ever make a profit with them or that you'll be able to time the market and sell at the top (the overwhelming majority of people don't). They do generally go up in value over time but again there is no guarantee that you'll get the timing right. They can be very volatile and in almost all cases are negative cash flow (similar to depreciating assets) while being held.

In the fourth quadrant are **Cash-Flow Assets**, which generate consistent income. Cash-flow assets are what the rich use to increase and compound their wealth year after year.

HOW THE RICH GET RICHER

So how do you structure your assets in such a way that the odds are in your favor? You do it by structuring your balance sheet to minimize your liabilities and maximize your assets, not unlike what people do in their personal lives. We all have strengths and weaknesses, but most successful people have figured out how to maximize their strengths and minimize their weaknesses. They focus on their assets and manage their liabilities (knowing they often can't be totally eliminated). The way you build financial wealth is exactly the same.

Once you start to generate surplus or discretionary income, you want to direct it into acquiring assets, which in turn will generate more cash flow. That's how "the rich get richer" and compound their wealth, and you'll want to do the same thing. *The ultra-wealthy are exceptionally good at using assets that tend to appreciate over time but produce current positive cash flow, or passive unearned income via rents, dividends, interest and royalties, or licensing fees.*

THE TWF WAY TO COMPOUNDING WEALTH

I have a client, a young guy in his mid-20s just starting out, who's focused on building a portfolio of rental real estate properties. He typically picks up foreclosures which require cash to close. He'll secure the financing up front, close the deal, make improvements to the property, then rent out the house. Each month the rent he receives covers his costs (mortgage, taxes, insurance, and maintenance) and then some, creating a positive cash flow. During the same time, the property appreciated in value by going from an unlivable foreclosure to pulling top dollar on the rental market. Now he has two options: he can compound the positive cash flow he receives each month, or he can choose to live off of it while the underlying asset, the property, continues to appreciate in value.

His options for compounding the cash flow include making other investments that pay dividends or acquiring another property. The important thing for him is not to eat, or spend, his seed, which in this case is the surplus money from the rental property. He has to replant it. He currently owns two cash-flow-positive properties and is working on his third. Instead of spending the money like many people would, he applies the True Wealth Formula and puts the money, the unearned-income profit from the two rental properties, into his Wealth account, which he then uses to buy investments that pay dividends and interest each month, fully automating growing his assets and cash flow even further. Instead of monthly profits from his rentals sitting dead doing nothing, it continues to compound month after month while he's out searching for the next deal to turn into a rental property. This is TWF methodology to a tee. It's not the only example of how to configure things, but it shows you *how to archi-*

tect a compound wealth-building machine, via the principles outlined in this book, and drive it to freedom.

DEFINING TRUE FINANCIAL FREEDOM

Cash-flow assets are generally passive in nature, and it's there that we want to put our focus, in the same ways the wealthy do. You increase your unearned income by building a strong and stable base of cash-flow assets. Once your base of cash-flow assets is solid, you're in a stronger position to take advantage of short-term opportunities to make quick money, to speculate in appreciating assets. For example: buying real estate when the market is low and selling when it is high, buying high-quality dividend-paying stocks during market crashes, or acquiring other high-quality distressed assets.

Your first goal is to get to a point where your unearned income is equal to your earned income. In TWF we call this your freedom number. That's when the crossover to financial independence begins: when you earn as much from your passive cash-flow investments as you do from your labor. Then if ever you aren't able to work for whatever reason, for a day or a week or a month, you have a stream of income. That's the goal. That's a position of strength. *That's true financial freedom.*

BALANCE SHEET INVENTORY

To build our fruit-yielding orchard that generates cash flow month after month, year after year, we need to first start by taking an inventory of where we are currently at. Start again by making a list of all of your assets and liabilities and identify those that are income-producing assets and those that are negative cash-flow assets.

Similar to the Income Pillar, the first thing on your list of assets will be your name. Other assets may include a rental property, a portfolio of dividend-paying stocks, bonds, or a secured loan you've made to someone who pays you interest. Other assets could be a CD (Certificate of Deposit), an interest-earning savings account.

Precious metals you have tucked away in a safe are technically considered assets, but they don't provide income. They are appreciating assets or speculations and generally have a negative-cash-flow characteristic similar to holding land. These are appreciating assets that cost you money to maintain and own, such as service fees, storage fees, transaction costs, rental fees, and taxes. Whatever they are, just get them all listed.

BALANCE SHEET

Assets (DA, AA, +CFA, L/NL)	Liabilities

On your list, make sure you've included *everything* and that you've left nothing out.

HOW TO BUILD A FORTRESS BALANCE SHEET

If you look at Fortune 500 companies like Apple or Microsoft, they have what's called in the financial industry "a fortress balance sheet." Their cash flows are enormous, and they have little debt and huge amounts of assets. Often they have significant intangible assets, such as intellectual property or goodwill in the marketplace, or they have capital-efficient assets, which are assets that rarely become obsolete. *Their balance sheets are extremely strong, which enables them to weather economic downturns, or even become stronger during them.* Their market share increases whether or not there's a recession or depression because their products are always in demand, which is why "blue chip" stocks often make an excellent addition to every investment portfolio when bought at the right time for the right reasons.

In TWF, we want to evaluate our balance sheets in a similar way, working to create one that's like a fortress, by reducing and eliminating negative-cash-flow assets and liabilities and maximizing positive-cash-flow assets.

GETTING YOUR MONEY'S WORTH FROM MISTAKES

Every failure is a learning experience and an important part of your financial education. When failure or mistakes happen, learn to extract the maximum value from them. I call this a tuition payment. *If you want to turn failure into an asset instead of a liability on your (mental) balance sheet, you have to learn how to make mistakes your slave.*

You do that by journaling and making sure you extract the maximum value out of every mistake that you can. You take full advantage of the situation by increasing your knowledge, improving your skills, attaining more experience, and expanding your contacts.

Even if your business fails, you'll have made valuable contacts that can help you in the future. One of them could lead you to a person who'll eventually become your next business partner, and the two of you go on to build a multimillion-dollar business together.

You never know where things will lead if you have the right mindset, a good strategy, and a positive approach to dealing with failure.

HOW TO CREATE A CLOSED-LOOP COMPOUND WEALTH MACHINE

Most people are stuck in a closed loop of income and expenses. They're trapped by their earned income going to feed their expenses. Usually, they're living above their means and have more debt than they should. This closed loop is a downward spiral that never ends. Income may go up over time, but expenses and debts rise too. When assets are acquired, they're typically negative cash flow (depreciating or speculative appreciating assets), leading to even more *earned-income* financial burden.

We want to restructure that closed loop so our income feeds our assets, and our assets feed our income. We do this by reducing expenses, increasing income, and feeding our assets with the difference. That's the essence of creating an asset-building wealth machine.

The assets on your balance sheet should generate

cash flow and increase your *unearned* income. As your income goes up and your debt goes down, you'll peel off the excess income to build your asset base. Instead of increasing your expenses and debt and buying *speculative* investments, which is what most people do, in TWF you focus on building your cash-flow assets. That's how you'll become an investor and not a gambler, *and it's also how you'll free yourself from the complexity and misinformation of the financial industry.*

When you follow the TWF model of restructuring your balance sheet for cash flow, momentum begins to build. I refer to this as an asset snowball or a compounding wealth machine, where *you literally have ever-increasing cash flow (income) each and every month due to the automation and compounding effect of how the assets are structured.* You and your family become very resilient or "anti-fragile" to market corrections, volatility, and chaos because your assets are covering your core nut, making you richer and freer every single month, quarter, and year. Again, this is how the "rich get richer."

When you do this, you start to become part of the "smart money" instead of the "dumb money," as Wall Street refers to it. You start to build up a *war chest of cash*, from a position of strength and power, able to "buy when there's blood in the streets." You can't do that if you're trapped in negative-cash-flow speculative financial products, dependent on "experts" to tell you what to do, and dependent on the stability of your personal earned income to pay their ongoing fees and expenses. There's just absolutely no real leverage or freedom in that model.

ND2 CAPITAL-ALLOCATION RULES

Now I want to show you how to manage the growing capital in your Wealth account and how to allocate your asset base for maximum safety, momentum, and growth.

Remember, in TWF we manage our money via ratios and formulas, not dollars and cents. We use *non-discretionary rules-based systems* the way the world's top investors, speculators, and wealthy do. Let's continue now and see how this strategy is applied to our Wealth account.

Recall that ND1, our 10/10/10/70% formula, is how we manage our *earned* income (the money we work for) to implement spending or consumption controls, get out of debt, and begin the wealth-building process.

ND2 (non-discretionary rules-based system #2) is our *capital-allocation model*, and it is our first top-level risk management formula for how we manage our *unearned* income (the money that works for us) or the capital in our Wealth account and other assets.

THINKING LIKE THE BANK

In True Wealth Formula, our ND2 system models the banking industry, the method of asset classification and capital allocation of the elites.

Tier One Assets (T1). Banks have what are called tier one assets, which are primarily cash or cash-like instruments. They're referred to as *liquid* assets. In TWF, we make sure that we have a healthy base of tier one assets.

Banks do stress tests and audits to determine their ability to handle a financial crisis by assessing their *tier one liquidity levels.* Around the world, governments have established varying requirements for banks to maintain healthy tier one asset levels ever since the global financial crisis in 2008.

In accounting terms, tier one assets are known as current assets. They tend to be short-term and liquid, or can be made liquid within twelve months. (Long-term assets in accounting terms are typically referred to as fixed assets.) High liquidity assets could be cash in a savings or money market account, short-term CDs, short-term government bonds, precious metals, or even crypto assets if held for the right reasons.

THE ROLE OF PRECIOUS METALS

Precious metals are highly liquid and have served as a store of value and money from the beginning of recorded history. Paper money, which was invented by the Chinese, was originally backed by a hard asset, such as silver or gold.

Paper money backed by faith alone in a government's credit is a newer invention. The change occurred in the United States in 1971 when President Nixon decoupled the US dollar from the gold standard. Prior to 1971, you could exchange a US dollar for gold or silver at a fixed rate of exchange.

The US dollar became the world's reserve currency as part of the Bretton Woods Agreement following the end of World War II. Because the United States was the strongest nation after the war and was willing to back its currency with precious metals, the world put its faith in the US dollar. This gave the US a big advantage in global trade and international financial transactions.

Other countries that didn't have the world's reserve currency were unable to print unlimited amounts of money.

Going off the gold standard was a major factor in why the United States went from being the world's largest creditor nation nearly 50 years ago to having the debt-based economy of today. It's a risky experiment and will likely end in a currency crisis (ultimately a crisis of trust) that leads to a new global world reserve currency system, again backed by hard assets to regain public faith and halt the ensuing chaos. Sadly, this is a repeating pattern throughout history.

Historically, central banks in particular, as well as the world's wealthiest families and countries, have kept a reserve of gold on hand or accessible as part of their T1 liquidity.

KEEP YOUR POWDER DRY

You want to maintain healthy tier one assets on your balance sheet because *all markets boom and bust*. You should always have access to cash, or what the investing world calls *dry powder*. You're gonna need dry powder the next time the market goes bust. That's the only way you'll be able to respond quickly to take advantage of the availability of good deals that become available when markets correct or collapse.

A famous investor once said: buy when there's blood in the streets. What this means is *the best time to buy is during a panic when people think the world as we know it is coming to an end, liquidity dries up, and asset values plummet*. You won't be able to seize those opportunities and "buy when there's blood in the streets" if you don't have tier one assets.

Typical financial advice suggests you keep some "emergency" cash handy, e.g., six months' living expenses. TWF lets you decide what this is. Obviously you want to have some emergency savings; that's just common sense. BUT the bigger picture and goal is your TWF Wealth account and how you are managing that capital. Your Wealth account is not a "savings account" that you rape and pillage whenever you want to buy something. It's not an "emergency fund" that you dip into every year or two when life gets a little difficult. And it's not for "retirement," at least not as retirement is defined by our modern society and culture. *It's to build your wealth machine and your legacy.* Will it provide for your retirement? Of course, but it should do much, much more.

When you follow the TWF model of focusing on cash-flow assets, you're not as dependent on an "emergency fund" because *you always have unearned income coming in.* Your focus becomes more about T1 liquidity ratios, dry powder, and chaos hedges—again, building that personal fortress balance sheet.

Tier Two Assets (T2). Tier two assets are your cash-flow assets, and they should make up the bulk of your holdings or net worth on your balance sheet. An example of a tier two asset is an established business that's consistently generating profit. It could be a primary business that provides you with a salary but also pays yearly profits, or one in which you are a passive investor or a limited partner. Again, the key characteristic of tier two assets is they produce consistent cash flow. They can be active or passive, but the goal is towards passive assets where we get leverage on our time.

Tier two assets may also be part of your core investment holdings, such as dividend-paying stocks, exchange-traded funds (ETFs), or closed-end funds (CEFs). They shouldn't be speculative investments. Blue-chip dividend-paying stocks, a portfolio of municipal bonds, short- or long-term government bonds, or corporate bonds could be tier two assets. Promissory notes, loans you make secured by an underlying asset (like a home mortgage secured by a First Deed of Trust on the underlying property), royalties, or licensing fees from intellectual property can also be tier two assets.

Tier Three Assets (T3). Tier three assets are appreciating assets and are *speculative* in nature. They may not generate income or dividends until sometime in the future, if at all, and may never contribute to your cash flow. They could be higher-risk growth stocks or real estate that goes up or down in value. Tier three assets have the potential for earning capital gains, which are subject to capital gains tax, but their value remains an unknown until you sell.

Some assets can be classified into more than one category, depending on what your intentions for the asset were when you acquired it. You could hold precious metals as part of your tier one asset base and if over time they go up in value, you could consider them a tier three asset. Or you may have a stock that pays dividends, but also appreciates in value over time. A company that pays dividends will most likely be classified as a tier two asset, but if you think the business has more potential for growth than paying income, you re-assign it to tier three. With experience, you'll learn how to best classify your assets.

A UNIQUE APPROACH TO ASSET ALLOCATION

We categorize assets into three tiers because we don't want to find ourselves in a situation where we have no liquidity or are unknowingly over-allocated towards risky and speculative negative-cash-flow assets. We always track and pay attention to our ND2 allocations. Start to think of your asset base like a bank, where you're the lender and no longer the borrower. This is core TWF thinking and mindset. By implementing these concepts, over time you'll also begin looking beyond yourself, to establishing a storehouse of resources for your family and community, and to building your legacy.

There's another reason we use our ND2 capital-allocation model. TWF looks at asset allocation differently than financial planners and the investment industry in general, which typically only take into account stocks, bonds, or insurance when making asset allocations. Most professionals aren't licensed and don't earn a commission selling "alternative" types of assets, so advice you get from conventional planners is typically limited to the stock market and doesn't account for other important assets like high-quality real estate, a successful cash-flowing business, or precious metals.

But our ND2 formulas do something beyond dealing with the broader range of asset allocation. *Unique to TWF, and largely because of the human-nature impact on investing results, ND2 helps us zero in on the dominant characteristic of the asset class itself and the primary reason for holding it on our balance sheet. This higher-level focus brings added safety, security, cash flow, and momentum to our wealth-building.*

HOW TO ALLOCATE BETWEEN T1, T2, AND T3

We typically provide the following default ND2 ratios, meaning this is how you might allocate the capital in your Wealth account as funds are building up. And it's how you begin the process of building an asset base that compounds and grows every month, making you richer every year instead of poorer.

- T1 cash and cash-like assets (liquidity): 10%
- T2 cash-flow assets (investments): 70%
- T3 appreciating assets (speculations): 20%

You'll notice some key phrasing used above: *liquidity, investments, speculations.* These terms are unique and central to TWF and our ND2 capital-allocation formulas. They make a clear distinction between key characteristics of the assets held, allowing us to begin the very important process of risk management.

When looking at your ND2 ratios, the biggest key with T3 speculations is to get your T1 liquidity then your T2 cash-flow assets set up first. Most people make the mistake of always chasing risky speculations (that they think are investments) and the statistics show that the majority of investors are absolutely terrible at timing the market. This is not by accident: it's because the financial industry sells products as "investments" which are really speculations or gambles. There is no training or focus on risk management even though that's the number one difference between a professional investor and amateurs.

Here's the key point: a wealthy person can swing for the fences and make a killing speculating precisely because he doesn't need the money! If it doesn't work out, he's got solid cash flow either from a high-paying career, successful business, or other core T2 investments. He's also got a safety net and healthy level of dry powder via his T1 liquidity ratios.

ND3 RISK MANAGEMENT RULES

True Wealth Formula is a system for becoming a successful self-directed investor. It's a master strategy to take responsibility for our finances, financial future, and wealth-building and not defer to someone else. It encourages each of us to accept responsibility for developing our money management and investment skills.

Part of taking responsibility entails making a clear-headed evaluation of your personal investing skills, which means you also have to assess your emotional temperament and tolerance for risk.

Some people are more risk-averse than others. A person who's uncomfortable with risk may have a high percentage of tier one assets and no tier three assets. Knowing your tolerance for risk as well as your aptitudes and skills will help you determine how to make financial decisions. You've worked hard for your money, so it's important to be honest with yourself about your comfort with risk and the knowledge you have.

Now we're going to explore some concepts and rules to help manage risk within individual portfolios and positions, meaning, we use ND2 for the big-picture capital allocation and risk management of our Wealth account. Then when we drill down into individual portfolios or positions of individual investments, our ND3 rules get even more specific.

FIVE CORE INVESTING RULES

I'm going to share five rules with you that—if you just applied these rules alone to your investment decisions—could save you from soul-crushing heartache. That may sound like an exaggeration, but it's not. If you only knew the price paid to learn these simple rules, and how following them with each and every investment decision you make can save you from catastrophic loss (a loss you literally do not recover from), you'd take them very seriously. *These rules make up the core foundation of our ND3 risk management formulas, and they should be memorized.*

Rule 1: Protect Your Capital

This classic rule seems like common sense, but it's the first rule in order to remind us to think carefully about the risks we're taking with our hard-earned money, and to make sure we've properly evaluated and understood all the risks involved when making an investment.

It doesn't mean that you'll never experience a loss. Indeed, one of the big differences between the professional investor and an amateur is that amateurs hate taking losses, so they ride a failing investment all the way down. Amateurs often sell at the bottom of a market cycle while professionals are methodical in determining when to cut their losses, get out of an investment, and move on to something else. *Professionals are willing to take small losses in order to avoid a big one.*

Protecting your capital is about respecting your capital. It's about knowing the price it took to save all that money and how much time it will take to replace it. It's about making sure you *avoid a catastrophic loss.* You need to know that when you make a decision for a specific investment, you're also making a decision against another investment. In other words, what is the value of money (and your time)? What other options are available out there? If I take on more risk than I should, why am I doing it? What is the real risk (vs perceived risk) of the investment? What alternatives do I have to (and what is the return on) this investment idea?

How to Work with an Advisor

The bottom line is to take complete personal responsibility for your financial affairs. It's worth repeating: *no one will do for you what you are not willing to do for yourself. If you don't protect your money, no one else will either.* Never assume a financial planner has your best interest in mind. He may be a nice guy with lots of experience and he may not be a crook, but when push comes to shove, human nature dictates he's going to look out for #1, which is himself and his family—which is exactly what you should be doing. Conflicts exist, and maintaining a healthy distrust and skepticism is critical to your financial survival, not ending up with an advisor who takes pleasure in "ripping their clients' faces off," as some money management firms embarrassingly disclosed during the global financial crisis.

If you're going to use a professional advisor, at least make sure they are a fiduciary (held to a higher legal standard). Also make sure you understand clearly how they make their money, what their business model is: is it fee-based, a percentage of assets under management (AUM), commissions, referrals, bonuses, or all of the above? Make sure everything is disclosed and that you understand it. I can't tell you how many times I've used "fiduciary" professionals who ended up using fee-based time to explain a financial product (sales pitch) that they make a commission on. *A good advisor is worth their weight in gold and worth every penny, especially if you don't want or don't have time to manage your own money, but they're not easy to find.*

One last thing: if you're going to hire an advisor, you have to stay engaged! You've got to be in their face, at least quarterly getting updated on what's going on, asking them questions and building a strong relationship. Learn to listen to what's not said and what's going on between the cracks, don't be afraid to ask them to explain things to you, and make sure you're reading the statements and reports and that they make sense. If they don't, call and ask questions! You must hold them accountable. NEVER, I repeat, NEVER let yourself think or feel that someone else who's smarter than you is going to protect you or your money more than you will (if they do, you got lucky; do not let your guard down). *Remember that keeping money and making it grow is a different skillset than making it, and part of that skillset is inspecting and holding advisors accountable.*

Rule 2: Invest in What You Know

The second rule is important. If you don't understand what you're about to do, don't do it. Never invest in something just because your best friend told you it was a good idea. Even if your professional advisor recommends putting money into a recommended fund based on your age, goals, and risk profile, be sure to *either understand what you're doing or minimize the investment down to the smallest possible "tuition payment" so you can get on the inside, go through your learning curve, and get a better understanding before scaling up.*

Realize that even if you think you understand an investment option, there's probably a lot more you don't know. Things are often not what they appear. We think we have 100 percent of the information or that our reasoning is sound and accurate, but that's generally not the case. There's always a larger number of unknowns than knowns when investing.

Mastering the Enemy Within

There is another factor to consider. The concept of risk cannot just be discussed in sterile modern-portfolio-theory terms. We actually don't know what our real risk tolerance is because we don't know what real risk is or how to measure it. More importantly, our human nature is always lurking, waiting to sabotage us. It's been said that there are 180 known cognitive biases. These are subconscious programs in the mind that have been developed and refined over thousands of years of evolutionary survival. Knowing something cognitively is not enough to counter these sub-programs. They are the default operating system, and they are just too powerful. Again, this is why when it comes to managing money and investing, using a non-discretionary rules-based system approach is a matter of life and death. Money literally represents the stored energy of your life.

The Truth about Risk or "Guaranteed Investments"

I have a close friend in the financial industry who is very, very smart. One day we got into a discussion about "zero risk" investments, and he was stating that a certain type of investment had no risk.

From a TWF perspective, there is no such thing as a guaranteed or risk-free investment. There is only real risk and perceived risk. When most people refer to no risk, what they are really saying is that there is no *perceived* risk.

Our human nature and biases (remember, there are 180 of them) tend to associate common and familiar activities, things that are endorsed by a perceived authority figure, or things we control (or believe we control) as low or no risk. However, we can have situations where there is low perceived risk but high real risk—or the opposite, where there is high perceived risk and low real risk.

Driving a vehicle is a perfect example. It is a relatively high-risk activity (with millions getting in car accidents each year) with very low perceived risk, because it's so common and familiar to us. Flying has high perceived risk, many people are terrified to fly, but statistically it has low real risk. This is because driving is common and familiar to most people (and you have a feeling of control while driving), while flying is not. The less familiar you are with flying, the higher your perceived risk (and fear) will be in contrast to someone who does it often. Neither of these extremes has anything to do with actual real risk. It is all perception.

An investing example of low perceived risk but high risk is when a market is peaking after years of growth (i.e., the 2007 real estate market), everyone you know is making money, and everywhere you look, the media headlines are confirming, "You can never lose money in real estate; they aren't making any more land, you know!" We tend to look to social signals to validate and confirm our biases, and when they do, it lowers our perceived risk. In this situation, the actual real risk is often much higher than we perceive.

The opposite is also true. After a market has crashed and bottomed out, people don't want to touch it because they got so burned in the last crash. Fear is still rampant, which keeps the perceived risk high, while the actual real risk is low (there isn't much downside left). This would be a form of recency bias, making us believe risk is higher (or lower) than it really is simply because it is what happened recently, when statistically the *probability* of the same event happening again so soon is very low. It's possible, but not probable. Managing risk is all about understanding and managing the differences between perception, probability, and possibility.

Here's another example. In my home island of Hawaii,

there is an active volcano. People build houses and neighborhoods on this volcano because there are specific areas where it hasn't erupted or threatened homes in decades. Perceived risk is low or muted because it hasn't happened recently. However, just last year, a mega-eruption happened and wiped out hundreds of homes. Fissures, or cracks in the earth, were literally opening up and spewing out lava in people's back yards! Now all of a sudden, people are freaking out because the worst has happened. But that real risk was always there. In fact, now that it just happened, the real risk is probably lower of it happening in that exact same area again, but perceived risk is now very high, and many people won't rebuild.

Remember this TWF rule: when it comes to investing, there is no such thing as no risk; there is only risk management.

There is always third-party counter risk, where another party may go bankrupt, not deliver on their promises, or manipulate market prices. Even FDIC insurance bank accounts have risk. Banks have become insolvent. Governments have gone bankrupt. It does happen. Not often, but it has in the past, and it will again with 100% certainty at some point in the future.

There is only one exception to this rule, and that is paying off your debt. If you have debt with an average interest rate of 10% and you pay it off early, every single dollar in interest you aren't paying to the lender is a guaranteed 10% return on your investment back into your pocket, not theirs. This is the only zero risk "investment" because the return is 100% known up front and 100% guaranteed.

In fact, some with large amounts of bad debt may want to consider a modified ND1 rule of 10/20/70, with 20% going towards debt acceleration and zero going towards Wealth account, until the debt is eliminated, then shifting the ratio back to 20% Wealth account where it should be to begin with.

You can use the proprietary calculators in our Wealth Builder app to determine which option is best, applying accelerated payments towards your debt or taking on risk via an investment (cash-flow asset or CFA) or speculation (appreciating asset or AA).

Rule 3: Start Small, Grow Big

Look for opportunities to start with small transactions. This can be easier to do with certain kinds of investments. For example, it's easy to open a brokerage account and buy a few shares of blue-chip dividend-paying stocks. It'll give you the opportunity to watch what happens over time and to note what makes the stock value go up or down. You'll gain experience with lower risk.

There's also little risk now to become a lender. Today you can easily start with peer-to-peer lending networks, where it's possible to open an account for as little as $25. Making loans to people and earning interest is a great opportunity to start small and grow big. It enables you to move from being on the outside to the inside of the financial system.

Keep a TWF journal and write down everything that happened during the loan so that when you make a mistake, you'll understand what went wrong and why. By learning everything you can and referring to your notes to guide future transactions, you'll extract the maximum educational value out of your experience. *Remember: you are the biggest asset on your balance sheet.*

Partnerships can offer another way to start small and grow big. They're an option for making real estate investments, owning rental properties, or starting a new business and give you the opportunity to learn from partners with more experience, which can reduce your risk.

As a general rule of thumb, always start with the smallest amount possible when you make a new investment. Chances are your first experience will be a learning one, so *you want to minimize the tuition and maximize the educational value*. I always consider a first investment as tuition payment. I never expect things to go well—maybe

I'll be defrauded, have inaccurate information, my timing is wrong, or I misunderstood something or had unrealistic expectations. By following this rule, it won't matter as much, because I'll have learned something valuable and minimized my tuition cost.

Rule 4: Allocate towards Cash Flow, Trend, or Value

Allocation refers to how you distribute your investments. It requires paying attention to what's going on with the investments on your balance sheet, whether they're positive cash flow, trending up or down, and what their fundamental valuations are. *Over time, most investments have a tendency to revert to the mean*, meaning they go through periods where they are either undervalued or overvalued. You want to be aware of market trends and conditions and when an asset class or sector becomes overheated (usually when everyone is talking about it and everyone thinks it's a good idea—e.g., circa 2007 "you can never lose money in real estate"—it's time to start scaling out and reallocate, or roll, your profits into another market or sector that is undervalued or starting a new uptrend).

How you allocate investments, whether in tier one, two, or three, will have a lot to do with your temperament. A general rule of thumb is to target 10 percent of your investments in tier one, 70 percent in tier two, and 20 percent for speculating. Your ratios may be different depending on your situation, but you keep your ND2 ratios in mind and rebalance as things change in the market.

How to Succeed as a Gambler

Remember this universal truth: *the house always wins*. So if you tend to find yourself attracted to speculative assets and gambles, how do you win and beat the house? You take money off the table, that's how. Our ND2 and ND3 rules automatically force you to do this.

In TWF, you set up non-discretionary checks and balances systems like you did to eliminate debt, especially if you have a tendency to speculate or gamble, so that you prevent your emotions from getting in the way. A person who likes to gamble would be wise to limit the percentage of his tier three allocations in his portfolio. No one wants to end up taking a big loss when there's volatility in the market.

For example, if you have a $100k portfolio and limit tier three speculations (capital gains investments with no cash flow and dependent on market timing to succeed) to a ratio of 20%, that's $20k. You've now capped your risk to a conservative level while still giving you an opportunity to capture profits from a rising market in an uptrend. If you're wrong, it's not a catastrophic loss. If you're right, you've increased your total available capital, and on the next go around, you'll have a new total with new ratios to work with. This forces you to exercise discipline in your investing and not just chase the "exciting" ideas which are usually the ones people lose money on. Remember, when it comes to investing, it's the boring stuff that often performs better over time with less risk.

If you have an asset that is inflating and becoming over-valued or more importantly, if the uptrend breaks down, consider rebalancing or selling part of it and putting that capital into an asset that is undervalued in order to maintain ND2 ratios on your balance sheet. You may also want to jump on a trend and ride it upwards if the asset is generating cash flow, undervalued, and/or in an uptrend. The rules you establish will guide your decisions.

Rule 5: Know Your Exit Strategy

Perhaps the thing that separates the pros from the amateurs more than anything else is having an exit plan. When most people invest, they rarely if ever think about how they'll get out of the investment. It's just as important to know when to sell as when to buy before you make any investment.

Make sure you know how you'll get out before you commit. If you enter a partnership and are excited about doing business with someone, plan your exit strategy too via a buy/sell clause. A partnership requires a different set of exit criteria than managing a portfolio of stocks. Each type of investment requires its own exit strategy. *Always ask yourself how and when you'll bring the investment to an end.*

For publicly traded securities like stocks, we use specific stop-loss strategies to give us our exit points. We pre-calculate that before ever entering the investment. For real estate, you're going to be looking at other things like gross rent multiplier ratios, interest rate trends, time on market, inventory ratios, and multiple offers or price drops as your indicators and exit strategies.

HOW TO COUNTER EMOTIONAL DECISIONS

If you follow the first four rules, particularly rules two and three, you'll be in a continual process of learning, which will give you additional knowledge for dealing with rules four and five. Having a system of non-discretionary rules helps override emotions that arise, especially if you get a stock tip at a cocktail party (exciting!) or happen to watch something discouraging on the news (depressing). Avoid emotional decisions based on fear or excitement.

Statistics show most individual investors make terrible decisions regarding their money, and professional money managers often don't do much better when fees are factored in. It's up to each one of us to educate ourselves and develop our own non-discretionary rules that govern how and when we invest.

KNOW THYSELF

There are many options for investing. The types of assets on your balance sheet don't have to be limited to stocks and bonds, as favored by traditional financial planning. People differ in temperament and lifestyle, and so do their balance sheets.

Stocks and bonds may be right for one person, while someone else prefers getting their "hands dirty" in something real and tangible like real estate. Maybe you have a family member with experience in municipal bonds who can help you manage a bond portfolio. Some assets are more complicated to manage than others and will appeal to a certain personality type. Freedom, security, and fulfillment vary from individual to individual and lead to different ways of investing and managing a balance sheet. Traditional financial planning and modern portfolio theory point everyone down the same path, regardless of personality, temperament, values, or lifestyle preferences.

True Wealth Formula looks at the big picture and puts the

individual investor in the center of the frame. It provides a model for learning about ourselves, our own personal temperament, skills, and emotional makeup, and becoming the master and commander of our ship. Even if we take experts on board, it's up to us to understand everything that's going on and to know how to ask the right questions of the experts. If something's off course, it's up to us to recognize it and make the correction. Even if we can't directly fix the problem, we're the ones responsible for identifying it.

REAL ESTATE FLIPS, RENTALS, NOTES, AND REITS

There are many ways to make money in real estate. One way is doing flips—buying a fixer-upper, renovating it, and selling it quickly. Doing flips successfully depends on a market that's going up and on having the insight to know when to buy and sell. It often (but not always) requires capital and an ability to crunch numbers so that you earn both a profit on your capital at risk PLUS pay yourself adequately for your time.

Flips can be profitable but risky! You can get caught on the wrong side of the market or inaccurately estimate costs to rehabilitate the property, and they can go bad. What happens if you can't do the flip and make money on the property? The best strategy in that scenario is to have a backup plan converting the flip into a solid rental property.

Our biggest flip ever was a property we owned in French Polynesia on what many consider the most beautiful island in the world, Bora Bora. The property was absolutely breathtaking with a private beach on Bora Bora's pristine lagoon, but it was a challenging experience with huge negative cash flows and more risk than we should have taken on. We sold to a billionaire and cleared seven figures' profit in just two years. The transaction itself, doing business with a billionaire, was extremely challenging and a learning experience that ended up shaping a lot of what TWF is today.

Rental properties are a good real estate investment for certain people. They can generate positive cash flow, have the potential for being an appreciating asset, and can also have tax advantages. But market conditions have to be right and can vary wildly in specific locations in order to be successful.

Lending money via a secured debt or a deed of trust is another way to participate in the real estate market. Consider this option only if you've already built a solid balance sheet and are starting to create your family bank (see next section). Then you'll be in the right position to make loans with promissory notes recorded against a piece of property as collateral. When lending, it's useful to have prior experience with rentals and flips in case your borrower defaults and the property forecloses. You may end up with a property instead of a promissory note on your balance sheet that you either need to rehab and rent or sell to get your money out.

A fourth way to make money in real estate is through real estate investment trusts (REITs). Often REITs are publicly traded companies with portfolios of loans or properties that are cash-flow positive. They typically distribute 90 percent of their profits to shareholders via dividends on a monthly basis. In certain market conditions they can offer a reliable yet passive way to participate in the real estate or lending market.

STOCK MARKET STRATEGY

With publicly traded stocks and bonds, there are three key things you need to know:

1. Fundamentals or valuations tell you WHAT to buy or sell.
2. Technical indicators like price, volume, and trend tell you WHEN to buy or sell.
3. Position sizing (how much to allocate into each individual investment or speculation) tells you HOW MUCH to buy or sell.

Fundamental data and valuations have to do with the underlying health of the company you're investing in.

Remember this, you're not trading stocks and bonds. You're buying a piece of a business. What do you know about that business? If I'm investing a small amount, I'm just testing the water or more focused on capitalizing on a trending market. The more I invest, the deeper diligence I do. I want to know about the company financials, balance sheet, cash flows, income statement, dividend payout ratios, capital efficiency, management track record, branding strength, and goodwill. I also want to consider its susceptibility to technological disruption. We use various sources to research this information when making decisions based on fundamental data and valuations.

How do you define a trend? In the stock market you can look at price and volume charts with moving average lines. The nine- and twenty-day moving averages show you the short-term trend, fifty-day moving averages give you the medium-term trend, and the 200-day moving average is the accepted long-term trend-line indicator. You also want to look for things like higher highs (uptrend) vs lower lows (downtrend), as well as breakouts (stocks making new all-time highs).

Remember nothing goes straight up or straight down, so you can have short-term trends within longer term trends. You can also have trading ranges where a stock is bouncing between different support and resistance price zones, which is essentially a consolidation or trendless state.

Often when stocks do this for some time, a breakout will eventually occur either to the upside or downside. Also remember that the overall trend of the broad market or sector is going to have the biggest impact on individual stocks as a whole. Meaning you can be in a solid stock with good fundamentals and in an uptrend, but if the general market goes into a correction or bear market, your stock is probably going to be heavily influenced by that overall market direction.

Position-sizing affects how much capital we allocate into an individual stock and is a critical aspect of our ND3 formulas for managing risk and diversifying. A simple rule to start with is the 5% rule. As an example, in a $100,000 portfolio you wouldn't have any more than $5,000 in any single position, spreading your risk across twenty different positions. A more advanced method is to use volatility-based position-sizing, essentially allocating more capital to less volatile, safer positions, and less capital to more volatile, riskier positions. This is the exact opposite of what most people do. Most people put more money into the most exciting "investments," over-allocating into speculations which often lead to heavy losses.

We have a detailed list of over 30 investment types rated by their returns and key characteristics available to members of our Wealth Builder app. The idea is to get you familiar with how to properly recognize investment options based on the TWF principles outlined in this book and to equip you to accurately distinguish between a speculation and an investment, as well as how to identify when you are being sold an investment "product" vs what the underlying asset really is.

A WORD ABOUT ASSET PROTECTION

Over time, as your Wealth account grows and your asset base or estate increases, it becomes important to protect yourself from threats like lawsuits. You'll want to consult with qualified advisors who specialize in asset protection. The specifics and characteristics of the types of assets you have on your balance sheet—businesses, properties, or other investments—will dictate the best asset-protection strategy. These may be entities (like trusts, LLCs, and Corporations) or insurance, or a combination of both. As already mentioned, tax planning is also an essential tool to protect the growth of your assets by making sure your affairs are structured to legally minimize your tax bite.

CHAPTER 6

LEGACY

THE BIG WHY

This chapter addresses what I call the big why: Why even bother using TWF to create a wealth-building machine? Why do we challenge ourselves to grow and learn new skills so that our value in the marketplace and ability to solve problems increase? Why do we embark on new ventures and start new businesses knowing the risk of failure is so high and can be so painful? Why do we control spending and limit consumption when the world around us says it's more fun to just show our wealth? Why do we produce more than we consume in order to save and invest the difference?

The answers to these questions lie at the heart of how and where we find validation and fulfillment in life. This section puts the concept of wealth into a bigger perspective and looks at how "true wealth" can provide purpose and meaning for future generations.

INTERNAL VS EXTERNAL FOCUS

In 1943, the psychologist Abraham Maslow developed a theory known as the hierarchy of needs in which he proposed that human beings are motivated by a range of needs. First is the basic need for food, shelter, and clothing. Then, all humans have a need for safety, followed by the need for close human relationships and love, achievement and respect from peers, and so on.

Ultimately, we seek personal fulfillment. Looking back at our chart in the Introduction, our higher needs are reflected in the top right quadrant of the Wealth Builder. It's there we want to focus our attention, on those things that bring us greater freedom, security, and fulfillment.

People who diligently apply the principles in this book can often achieve a significant level of financial freedom and security within a few years. Achieving fulfillment can take longer, but it can start right now. Like a spiritual journey, it's an inner game. We arrive at some point in our lives, hopefully sooner rather than later, when we begin to focus on others more than ourselves and prioritize our relationships, whether with others in our life, with our community, with our country, or with a philanthropic vision for doing good works.

TWF values maintaining healthy relationships and contributing to the lives of others in productive ways because ultimately we're not taking any of this material wealth with us. It's the relationships in our life that make or break our level of true fulfillment.

RETIREMENT VS LEGACY

Most of the focus in our culture and modern financial planning today is on retirement, which is really another form of self-focus. Many people are finding that retirement isn't all it's cracked up to be. Without sufficient money or something to do, they become unhappy. Someone who's worked a job they hated for 50 to 60 hours a week their entire lives may feel differently, but to someone who's had a productive work life, contributed to society, and created value, this modern concept of retirement may not be as attractive.

Rather than focus on retirement, TWF is about creating a legacy. Legacy is why we do what we do, and it has nothing to do with how old we are, although it's natural to start thinking about such things later in life.

Now I will do my best to explain the process of how to

implement TWF Legacy. Keep in mind that while I wrote this book and while I've spent years researching and working through the processes of this topic, I consider myself no expert on such things. This should be considered a summary overview and orientation of just some of the core ideas, not an execution manual. As I've mentioned before, I am not an attorney, CPA, or certified financial planner, and you should always consult a qualified professional for anything related to estate or tax planning. Remember, we didn't come from wealth or an educated family. Inside, I'm still just an uneducated beach kid from Hawaii doing my best to try and figure this stuff out. I remind our family and business clients often: this is an experiment; we are deep in our own learning process! There are no guarantees, but at least we have a shot and we have the right picture to model ourselves after to increase our chances of success.

With that understanding, let's continue learning about the Legacy model.

THE BLESSING AND CURSE OF WEALTH

There's an interesting correlation between family and wealth. It's been correctly observed that inherited wealth can be the most destructive thing to family. Ironically, family (due to disagreements, fighting, lawsuits, lack of knowledge, and overconsumption) is often the most destructive thing to inherited wealth. Family has the potential to destroy wealth as much as lawsuits, poor estate and tax planning, poor money management, failed investments, wars, and other crises. And inherited wealth can be just as destructive to family as abuse and drugs.

When wealth comes with no strings attached, it creates entitlement and dependency that robs the next generation of the blessing of hard work and accomplishment, a desire to grow and fail, and the chance to learn from mistakes. Wealth without responsibility can be deadly to a person's self-esteem and sense of fulfillment and divide rather than unite a family through bickering and lawsuits, which can consume large sums of money.

MODERN ESTATE PLANNING VS BUILDING A LEGACY

There are three traditional approaches for dealing with the transfer of wealth at the end of a lifetime. One is the inheritance model, which is the most common. I call it the *die-and-distribute* model: when you die, you distribute your estate to your heirs and beneficiaries.

The second model is the charity model. Sometimes wealthy individuals don't want to pass their wealth onto their heirs, so they set up a foundation or leave their estate to the local church. They give away all of their wealth.

The third option is the spend-it model. Think of the popular bumper sticker that says: I'm spending my children's inheritance! It expresses the values of much of Western culture these days.

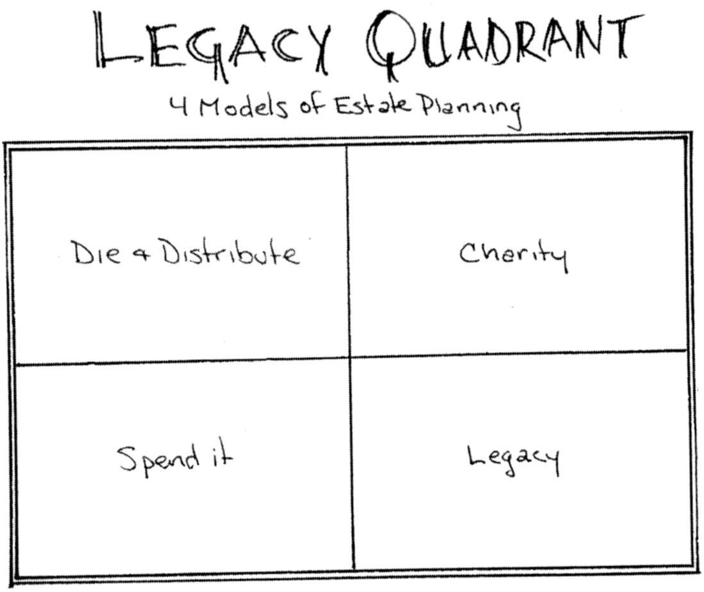

There are problems with each of these three approaches. Passing wealth on in the die-and-distribute model without also passing on the knowledge and character necessary for managing wealth can be destructive. The give-it-all-away charitable model can end up "giving a fish" instead of "teaching how to fish" and create dependency. It may inadvertently reinforce the habit of looking to others for resources to survive. Also, it's not uncommon that a large percentage of charitable organizations' funds go towards operations, not distribution. The spend-it-all-before-you-die approach is the ultimate in self-centeredness. Nothing is left behind. Your only legacy is that you were a fantastic consumer, and then you died.

The Legacy model is a fourth option, and it challenges us to consider something greater than ourselves. There's an old proverb that says a good man leaves an inheritance to his children's children. The TWF model is concerned not only with how much wealth you pass on but *how and when you do it*—when to inform the next generation about family assets and how to provide opportunities for developing the character and skills to manage wealth without ruining ambition.

BUILDING A LEGACY STARTS WITH YOUR VALUES

Both my wife and I grew up in poor, dysfunctional families. We became entrepreneurs at an early age and built successful businesses, and we made lots of mistakes and learned many lessons along the way. We didn't want the same thing for our kids (meaning we didn't want them to grow up poor with no security and an unstable environment, having to survive on streets, etc.) We wanted to raise our children in a stable family and give them a very different upbringing than ours.

At the same time, we didn't want our kids to get everything they desired. We wanted them to learn the value of hard work and started them working in our business at early ages. From the time they were nine or ten years old (and younger), we taught them to work and save money.

We also wanted our kids to appreciate the simple things in life. A passage from Ecclesiastes written by Solomon, who was the wealthiest and wisest king on earth, captures the sentiment: "Then I looked on all the works that my hands had wrought, and on the labor that I had labored to do: and, behold, all was vanity and vexation of spirit, and there was no profit under the sun."

Our goal was to use our resources to help prepare the next generation to be successful, productive members of society and to continue contributing to the *collective family balance sheet*. We are focused on building a legacy so that whatever wealth the family has doesn't destroy our family.

A side note: you may think it takes a lot of money to ruin people or create chaos in a family, but I can't tell you how many times I've seen siblings or heirs fighting over the smallest of things when someone in the family passes without a will, trust, or clear instructions. But it's even worse when there is no unifying value system and culture within the family. So please understand when I'm talking about "wealth" here, in TWF terms what we're really talking about is your legacy—the example you set, the character, skills, and *value system* that you pass on to the next generation—as much as or more than money, resources, and assets.

MODELING MULTIGENERATIONAL SUCCESS

TWF is not too keen on the "die and distribute" model or "inheritance" as defined by Western culture. We prefer to define it more broadly. Instead, we are adopting a "family bank" concept to help our kids build their own balance sheets and create opportunities for them to learn how to do the same.

TWF Legacy model adopts a family office/family counsel model where the family, as they age and mature, are more and more involved in management of certain family assets. When we're gone, their responsibility will be to the next generation below them, not to themselves. They are not the beneficiaries (directly) but they act as *custodians* who have a responsibility to the beneficiaries which are the successive future generations.

Many of the world's most successful families use the legacy model. *It's actually been around since the beginning of time and is the longest-standing method of intergenerational tangible and intangible asset transfer*. Multigenerational families are able to compound returns on their specialized knowledge, whether from their business, their contacts, or both. The idea is that future generations don't begin at zero and can leverage what the previous generation created. The legacy model encourages a culture that values personal responsibility, achievement, and hard work. It's geared towards creating producers not consumers of wealth.

THE FAMILY OFFICE CONCEPT

According to the legacy model, every family member funds his or her own lifestyle. This is critical to the model's success and keeps family members hungry and eager for new opportunities. No one relies on the family wealth for day-to-day living. Each member has to go out and work, produce, and create value in the marketplace. Everyone applies the principles and strategies of TWF for him- or herself and generates their own earned income, learning to produce more than they consume and build up capital and assets in their Wealth account.

If a member of the family wants to live in a bigger house, then he has to work for it. If she wants to drive a nicer car, she's got to earn the money to pay for it. Essentially, the legacy model puts strings or strict conditions on family money. The intent is to establish controls and protocols that regulate how capital is dispersed and to limit distributions to the right kinds of projects only, i.e., cash-flow assets. This helps each family member be productive and achieve their own success in life.

The mechanism for implementing these principles is via the concept of the "family office." The ultra-wealthy have been using some form of the family office for decades. Setting up a family office does require a *significant amount* of wealth, expertise, and resources to implement and manage, but there are some things anyone can do now to implement this model into their family regardless of how wealthy they are.

The family office is a method for holding on to family wealth by "institutionalizing" decision-making—in other words, running it like a business. It helps keep the family together and united through shared financial interests, and it helps future generations by making resources available to them without robbing them of the opportunity to work for their own success in life. It uses the same principles that have helped business-owning families hold onto wealth for generations. Like a corporation, a family office could theoretically last forever.

The Italians are particularly good at creating successful family offices. Beretta, which is one of the top firearm brands in the world, is owned by an Italian family that's been in business for over 200 years. Many Italian wineries and fashion houses are also multi-generational family businesses. You see this model applied throughout Europe and other places too, often referred to as "old money."

THE FAMILY COUNCIL

A family office should include a set of organizational structures, similar to businesses which typically have a board of directors that oversees operations, management, procedures, and protocols for how decisions are made, money is spent, and investments are chosen. They have mission statements and a set of values. A family office has many of these same structures, including a logo, or in the case of old-world families, a family crest or coat of arms. Another component of the family office is the family council, which is the equivalent of a corporate board of directors.

The family council is the governing body of the family estate. It's responsible for decisions concerning the management of family assets as well as directing all disbursements of money. In order to sit on the family council, a family member has to be engaged in some form of productive activity and making a significant contribution to the family.

The family council distributes money according to the

stipulations of the family trust, whether it's for education, career advancement, or more likely via financing operations of the family bank towards cash-flow assets. Family resources, or seed money, are managed for the benefit of future, not current, generations, and to contribute to the family's financial stability. The family council doesn't give handouts or bailouts, and no one can serve on the council for self-gain.

In our own family, as we're experimenting and learning how to apply this model (again, keep in mind we weren't born or raised wealthy—we are learning this as we go), we've found it's good to get kids involved early in the "family council" meetings, even if they're unable to vote (initially only the wealth creators—often the first generation of wealth—would have the power to vote or would retain a veto power). The goal is to have the entire family participating in the process and learning together for years so that by the time the initial wealth creator(s) pass on, the council is well established and skilled in managing the family's estate as the second generation is taking over and leading without the input or direction of the first generation.

A key objective of a family office is to help current and future family members find meaningful purpose in life and discover a path that brings them freedom, security, and fulfillment. This is how a family legacy can continue and endure for generations. Providing opportunities for lifelong learning helps ensure resources are properly used for passing on family values and wealth.

A word of caution: this is no small project, especially if you're a first generation figuring out the model by trial and error. It takes time to work out the details of how to structure a family office, to determine criteria for serving as a member of the family council, and all the other components that make it work. There's a reason why this has traditionally only been used by the world's ultra-wealthy—it's not easy. Keep in mind the TWF principle *start small, grow big*. Also, there is a reality in that you are dealing with different people, personality types, interests, motivations, commitment levels, and above all, *free will which must be honored*. Give yourself grace to make adjustments and tweaks over time as your family grows.

TRUSTS AND THE FAMILY BANK

Most people think trusts are only for large estates or for rich people, but that's not true. No matter how large or small an estate is, it makes sense to set up a trust, and it's certainly a key component of the Legacy model.

There are two types of trusts. The first one to set up is a revocable trust, which is what most living trusts and family trusts are. It is a foundational component of estate planning that includes a will and covers healthcare and other directives. The other type of trust is an irrevocable trust, which is more dynastic or permanent in nature. These types of trust require an experienced attorney to structure them properly and make sure they are drafted to meet the values and goals of the family as well as incorporating efficient tax planning.

Trusts typically have a specific purpose, whether it's to fund education, support humanitarian work, or start new business ventures. A trust can also include a "family bank," which stipulates how money will be managed. The family bank could be a brokerage account, a bank account, an LLC, or other entity that holds assets owned by the trust. In TWF, the assets of the trust are those that have been growing over the years in the Wealth account. The trust becomes the owner of the Wealth account, which has now likely grown into multiple assets, so that when the original wealth creators die, the family wealth is preserved.

The family bank functions as a means for setting aside a portion of the trust's assets for the benefit of the family office. It makes capital available for worthwhile, productive activities.

Let's say a family member is young, working full time, covering all of his or her responsibilities, and wants to begin building a portfolio of rental properties. In order to scoop up the type of properties that are good for fixing up and renting, he needs cash, which can be hard to lay your hands on when you're starting out in life. That's when a family bank could step in and make a loan. Ideally, by the time that happens, the family office is well established and the family member who wants the loan has assimilated family values and has no consumer or depreciating asset debt.

If a family member who receives a loan doesn't fulfill his or her responsibilities or fails to keep up with payments on the note, the family bank will foreclose on the property and take it over, like any bank would.

A family bank could also give loans for starting a business. Before doing so, the bank would look closely at the history and skillset of the family member who seeks the loan to determine if there's a good chance the business venture will succeed, but it will never give a handout. The family bank could also choose to fund education, either through a grant or a loan. If a family member uses the education in a productive way, the loan can be forgiven or converted to a grant, but it's better if the family member pays it back knowing he's contributing to the value of the family bank for future generations. There is flexibility, but *a family bank's primary goal is to serve future generations, and that requires the balance sheet to remain solvent and healthy.*

ANNUAL FAMILY MEETINGS

Annual family meetings bring the family together once a year (or more) to talk about the family's assets, its businesses and properties, and the investments of the family bank.

We started having family meetings when our kids were young. It offered us a way to begin teaching them the value of honest and diligent work, how to manage money, the differences between good and bad debt, what's involved in making investments, and the other TWF concepts and principles. We instilled in them the values that were meaningful to the family and encouraged our kids to find their purpose and their own path to success and fulfillment in their lives. We also discussed the importance of their success so they could contribute to the family wealth on behalf of their kids and grandkids.

Annual meetings also provide a format for dealing with family challenges or conflicts, which are more important to deal with than money. Every family goes through challenging situations, whether there are health issues, personality conflicts, substance abuse, low self-esteem, debts, lawsuits, or divorce. Life is full of ups and downs. The family meeting offers an opportunity for fleshing out issues that would otherwise remain buried and could lead to divisions in the family. The family office is about creating unity, and the annual meeting is a great opportunity to come together.

A family meeting could begin with a discussion of the family's investments and financial decisions. It could also include educational sessions (by family members or by inviting outside guests or experts) on relevant topics, such as strategies for investing or property management techniques. Then time can be set aside to talk about other matters, like a problem someone may be having with a teenage kid.

It goes without saying that a family meeting is an excellent excuse to get together and have a good time. Sometimes we've held our family meetings in a foreign country; other times we go to a fun destination nearby. It could even be as simple as "roughing it" via a camping trip. Sometimes we may only spend a few hours discussing family business. The rest of the time, we hang out, enjoy each other, and have fun.

FAMILY CULTURE

Often when people think of their legacy, they think about traditional estate planning, which typically entails setting up a trust and preparing a will. There's little consideration given to family values and perpetuating the family culture, nor any requirement that the family gather once a year to discuss family matters.

Family culture includes leadership styles, traditions, and

shared values including faith issues. It may emphasize giving, education, or physical fitness and well-being. Family culture includes celebrations like birthdays, holidays, vacations, and other types of get-togethers. Our family meetings have become an important part of our family culture. Even the grandkids look forward to them. Obviously, the younger kids don't participate in family council meetings, but they're with everyone for a week and have fun with their cousins.

The family culture unites family members around common values and resources, such as specialized knowledge, experience, contacts, and spiritual wisdom, as well as assets in the family bank. The family has a reason to stick together and work through challenges because of shared interests and values both tangible and intangible.

A strong family grows generation after generation. Each new generation taps into the assets, resources, and advantages of the prior one. As the family grows, it can reach out to other families and to the community. Each member of the family is free to pursue his or her passion, whether it's doing charitable work, being an entrepreneur, or working as an employee. It's all good. Diversity and difference are part of the family's strength, not a weakness. Family members may not always like each other or agree on everything, but they're united by shared concerns.

True Wealth Formula encourages you to start working on creating a lasting legacy as soon as possible. Like anything else, there'll be a learning curve and mistakes will be made. It could take up to ten or twenty years or more to fine-tune the components and processes involved, like with any business. It'll take time to find out what works and what doesn't. After procedures are standardized and family culture is institutionalized, the legacy structure takes on a life of its own.

Statistically, more than 90% of all wealth is destroyed within three generations, meaning that wealth in all its forms is almost always consumed within three generations of its original creation. So the goal of the Legacy model is to help put odds in our favor of resolving the negative consequences associated with wealth. Again, we have no guarantees of success but it's my sincerest belief that this model gives us the best percentage shot, while at the same time giving our families a productive and interesting project to work on together! And that all by itself is worth it.

CONCLUSION

True Wealth Formula is about much more than money; it's a mindset and way of living a blessed life. In addition to providing tools and techniques for creating financial independence and security in life, it values and supports maintaining positive relationships, good health, and spiritual strength.

Adopting TWF means embarking on a life of self-discovery and learning from adversity. The goal is to become a stronger, better, more fulfilled person on the road to acquiring wealth.

No one wants to end up being the Rich Miserable Bastard. Too often people hurt others in the pursuit of wealth. They scam people, take advantage of them, defraud the system, use corruption, and step on others to advance themselves and acquire money. Or they're constantly seeking more wealth, more success, more power, or more prestige. They're never happy or fulfilled and lack meaningful quality relationships in their lives.

True Wealth Formula places a high priority on the quality of life and the pursuit of freedom, security, and fulfillment. Freedom and security come as much from healthy relationships as from financial resources, and fulfillment stems from making a positive contribution to society, having a close relationship with the Creator, and *knowing who we are. Ultimately, true wealth lies in the heart. It's something money can't buy.*

When I started on my journey searching for wealth, I reached a point where nothing I was encountering provided the fulfillment I was seeking. I was unhappy and not always treating people how I would have liked to. Others' opinions of me were affecting how I felt about myself. I was only looking at external things to make me happy—at numbers, outward success, progress, and achievements—instead of looking within. Even today, this enemy within sometimes raises its ugly head and requires eternal diligence.

Many people mistakenly believe they have to choose between having money or being loved by God. What matters is how we use our time and energy. If we value material goods more than people, we'll abuse people to get what we want. If we value relationships with others but think ambition and success are bad, our own results will be sabotaged. According to TWF, we can have both at the same time. We have a choice, if we're willing to take responsibility for ourselves, to create value for others, and live by the law of Love.

It's my hope that this book will help you discover that true wealth means inner wealth. True wealth comes from the heart and spiritual strength from the Creator. When you understand that, then all the resources you'll ever need will be available for creating your legacy!

NEXT STEPS?

If you enjoyed this book and want to continue mastering True Wealth Formula, visit www.TrueWealthFormula.com/book and:

- Join our community of Wealth Builders by downloading our mobile app.
- Subscribe to one of our implementation or coaching programs.
- Share or gift this book with others you want to make an impact on.
- Send me your comments or testimony; I would love to hear from you!

ABOUT THE AUTHOR

HANS JOHNSON rose from a childhood of poverty to become co-founder and chief executive of a multimillion-dollar business. Raised in Hawaii, Hans started his first business at the age of eight, learning through self-study, innate curiosity, and the desire to transcend his circumstances. By the time he was twenty-three, he was featured in *Success* magazine for earning a six-figure income as the owner of a home business. Today, he is the developer of the True Wealth Formula system and Wealth Builder app, available in app stores. Hans lives in Texas with his wife, inspirational speaker Dani Johnson.